How to Write and Use
Instructional Objectives

How to Write and Use Instructional Objectives

Sixth Edition

Norman E. Gronlund

Professor Emeritus
University of Illinois at Urbana-Champaign

Merrill,
an imprint of Prentice Hall

Upper Saddle River, New Jersey   *Columbus, Ohio*

Library of Congress Cataloging-In-Publication Data

Gronlund, Norman Edward
How to write and use instructional objectives / Norman E. Gronlund.—6th Ed.
p. cm.
Includes bibliographical references (p.) and index.
ISBN 0-13-886533-7
1. Lesson Planning. 2. Education—Aims and Objectives.   I. Title.
LB1027.4.G76   2000
371.3'028—dc21   98-32378
                                                                              CIP

Cover Photo: Tony Stone
Executive Editor: Kevin M. Davis
Production Editor: Julie Peters
Text Designer: Andrea Reider
Cover Designer: Curt Besser
Design Coordinator: Diane Lorenzo
Production Manager: Laura Messerly
Electronic Text Management: Marilyn Wilson Phelps, Tracey Ward, Karen L. Bretz,
    Melanie King
Director of Marketing: Kevin M. Flanagan
Marketing Manager: Meghan McCauley
Marketing Coordinator: Krista Groshong

This book was set in Transitional 521 by Prentice Hall and was printed and bound
by R.R. Donnelley & Sons Company. The cover was printed by Phoenix Color Corp.

© 2000 by Prentice-Hall Inc.
Pearson Education
Upper Saddle River, New Jersey 07632

Earlier editions, titled *Stating Objectives for Classroom Instruction*, © 1978 and 1985 by
Norman E. Gronlund; *Stating Behavioral Objectives for Classroom Instruction* © 1970 by
Macmillan Publishing Company; *How to Write and Use Instructional Objectives*, © 1991,
1995 by Macmillan College Publishing Company.

Printed in the United States of America

10 9 8 7 6 5 4 3 2 1

ISBN 0-13-886533-7

Prentice Hall International (UK) Limited, *London*
Prentice Hall of Australia Pty. Limited, *Sydney*
Prentice Hall Canada Inc., *Toronto*
Prentice Hall Hispanoamericana, S.A., *Mexico*
Prentice Hall of India Private Limited, *New Delhi*
Prentice Hall of Japan, Inc., *Tokyo*
Prentice-Hall (Singapore) Pte. Ltd., *Singapore*
Editora Prentice Hall Do Brasil, Ltda., *Rio De Janeiro*

To
Marie Ann Cronlund
and
Erik, Derek, and David

Preface

As with earlier editions, this book describes and illustrates how to state instructional objectives in performance terms, and how to use them in teaching, learning, and assessment. The procedure is adaptable to all types of intended learning outcomes, ranging from simple to complex, and to all levels of instruction. The method is especially useful for describing those complex outcomes that are difficult to define, such as thinking, problem solving, and various types of performance skills. As schools move from a focus on overly specific tasks to more comprehensive and integrated tasks, there is a need for statements of instructional objectives that can clearly describe these broader learning outcomes.

Part I describes how to write instructional objectives as intended learning outcomes so that they convey the types of student performance to be demonstrated as a result of learning. It also includes a chapter on how to begin preparing a list of objectives for instruction. Self-checks are used to enable you to determine how well you understand the procedure for stating objectives.

Part II focuses on writing objectives for intellectual, affective, and performance outcomes. One chapter discusses objectives for higher-level thinking skills and two chapters focus on performance objectives—one on performance skills and one on problem solving.

Part III describes how to use objectives in teaching, testing, and performance and affective assessment. Here the emphasis is on how objectives, stated as intended learning outcomes, can play an important role in all aspects of the instructional process.

New to This Edition

This sixth edition has been revised from the last edition in a number of ways. Some of the more important changes include the following:

1. Chapter 1 was expanded to describe in more detail the reasons objectives should be used in instruction.
2. Chapters 2 and 3 were combined and revised to make the process of writing objectives clearer.
3. Chapters 4 and 10 were combined and rewritten as Chapter 3 to focus earlier on how to get started in preparing a set of objectives for instruction.

4. Chapters 5 and 6 were combined and reworked as Chapter 4, to highlight the differences between objectives at the knowledge, comprehension, and application levels.

5. A new chapter on writing performance objectives for problem-solving projects was added (Chapter 8).

6. Chapter 12 on assessing learning was divided into two chapters, one on achievement testing (Chapter 10) and one on performance and affective assessment (Chapter 11).

7. New descriptions of objectives, new sets of guidelines for preparing and using objectives, and new illustrations were added to several of the chapters.

These changes should make the book a more useful guide for writing instructional objectives for all types of intended learning outcomes, and for using them to improve student learning.

My special thanks to reviewers of the fifth edition who made valuable suggestions: Grace Callaway, Georgia College; Martha A. Drobnak, West Chester University; and Kathleen S. Whittier, Plattsburg State University. I'm also appreciative for the comments provided by reviewers of the current edition: Susan M. Brookhart, Duquesne University; Kathryne Newton, Purdue University; John A. Sanderson, University of Virginia; Rebecca B. Saunders, The University of North Carolina at Greensboro; and Charles K. West, University of Illinois at Urbana-Champaign. Thanks also go to Calvin K. Claus for the list of verbs in Appendix C, to the editorial staff of Merrill/Prentice Hall, and to Irene Palmer for excellent typing.

N. E. G.

Contents

Part I

How to Write Instructional Objectives

Chapter 1

Writing Instructional Objectives as Intended Learning Outcomes

After reading this chapter, you should be able to[1]

1. Describe what is meant by stating instructional objectives as intended learning outcomes.
2. Describe the advantages of using instructional objectives that are stated as intended learning outcomes.
3. Distinguish between objectives stated as learning outcomes and those stated in terms of the teaching process or the learning process.
4. Explain why it is desirable to include both general objectives and specific learning outcomes when writing instructional objectives.
5. State reasons for not including conditions and standards when writing instructional objectives.

When planning for instruction, teachers typically focus on the selection of content, teaching method, and instructional materials. These are all important elements of instructional planning, but the entire process is more effective if attention is first directed toward instructional objectives.

What Are Instructional Objectives?

In the past, instructional objectives have been stated in many ways and have focused on various aspects of instruction (e.g., teaching procedures, learning process, instructional

---

[1]These objectives are stated as intended outcomes, but because of space limitations, they do not follow the preferred two-step process described throughout this book. However, they should provide a satisfactory guide for study.

content, student performance). Here we shall describe instructional objectives as intended learning outcomes, that is, in terms of the types of performance students are able to demonstrate at the end of instruction to show that they have learned what was expected of them. Well-stated objectives clarify these expectations in terms of measurable or observable student performance.

The intended outcomes of education can be put in broad terms as is necessary in stating national, state, or local program goals (e.g., Develops proficiency in Basic Skills), or they can be stated as specific learning tasks (e.g., Writes a complete sentence). The following diagram presents a continuum of educational outcomes in terms of their specificity.

Figure 1.1   Levels of Intended Educational Outcomes

National goals	State goals	Local program goals	Classroom instructional objectives	Specific learning tasks
1	2	3	4	5

Our focus will be on Level 4, Classroom Instructional Objectives (e.g., Demonstrates writing skill). This level of specificity provides a focus for teaching, learning, and assessment without restricting a teacher's flexibility in selecting instructional methods and materials. The broad goals on the left side of the diagram provide a framework for curriculum building and for identifying classroom instructional objectives, but they are stated in terms that are too general for direct use in teaching. The specific learning tasks on the right side of the diagram might be useful for listing learning outcomes in a training program and for some simple outcomes in classroom instruction, but they are too specific for most instructional uses. When used with complex learning outcomes, they result in long, unmanageable lists that limit teaching to a lockstep system and neglect the integration and transfer of learning. With the increasing emphasis in education on reasoning and problem solving, performance skills, the application of learning to "real-life" situations, and other complex learning outcomes, the listing of specific tasks is inadequate for describing the vast array of intended outcomes of instruction.

What is needed for most classroom instruction is a limited, manageable set of instructional objectives, with each objective defined by a list of specific types of performance that students are able to demonstrate when they have achieved the objective. This enables us to describe intended learning outcomes ranging from simple to complex, and provides us the freedom to use a variety of instructional methods and materials to help students achieve the objectives.

The specific learning tasks used in classroom instruction are, of course, derived from the objectives, but they typically provide the means to an end rather than serve as ends in themselves. For example, we may teach students new vocabulary but the intended outcome is improved reading, writing, or speaking and not simply increased vocabulary. Similarly, we might teach certain number operations but our achievement target may be understanding mathematical concepts, problem solving, or mathematical reasoning. Thus, the instructional objectives provide the focus for instruction and the specific learning tasks provide the activities designed to achieve the intended outcomes. With simple learning outcomes the objectives and tasks may be similar, but with complex learning outcomes they are likely to differ considerably.

Why Use Instructional Objectives?

When instructional objectives are properly stated as intended learning outcomes—that is, in terms of the types of student performance we are willing to accept as evidence of learning—they serve a number of useful purposes, as shown below.

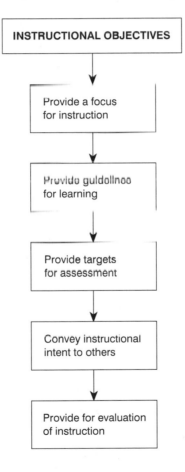

Role of Objectives in Teaching

A clear statement of instructional objectives provides a focus that results in more effective instructional planning, teaching procedures, and learning assessment.

Instructional planning too frequently focuses on the methods and materials of instruction without a clear conception of how students are to demonstrate what they have learned. As a result, the instruction and the assessment of learning focus primarily on knowledge outcomes, to the neglect of higher-level learning outcomes (e.g., thinking skills and complex performance skills).

By clearly stating our instructional objectives as intended learning outcomes, we provide a basis for selecting the methods and materials of instruction that are most likely to bring about the desired changes. If we want students to be able to apply what they are learning, we have to provide experiences that call for application. If we want students to think critically, we have to select materials that require critical thinking. If we want students to be able to solve complex problems like those in the "real world," we have to focus on more realistic performance activities. Well-stated instructional objectives provide a framework for planning an instructional program that focuses on the changes we want to bring about in our students.

Instructional objectives also provide a basis for integrating teaching, learning, and assessment. These should all be in close harmony. For example, we teach students problem-solving skills, students learn by solving problems, we check their learning by having them solve problems. Similarly we teach students how to write, have them practice writing, and we assess them by having them write something. In both cases we focus on the intended outcomes—problem-solving ability and writing ability. We don't give them a test to see if they *know* how to do it, we actually have them demonstrate their skills. Instructional objectives provide this type of focus needed for integrating teaching, learning, and assessment.

Instructional objectives also provide a basis for checking learning progress and providing feedback to students. If we describe our intended outcomes clearly enough, we can pinpoint learning strengths and weaknesses and provide students with timely and clear guides for improving learning. For example, if problem-solving outcomes are described in sufficient detail, we can determine whether students can distinguish between accurate and inaccurate data, facts and opinions, or relevant and irrelevant events. If not, we can plan remedial work to overcome the deficiencies.

Role of Objectives in Student Learning

If instructional objectives are shared with students at the beginning of instruction, they provide students with clear achievement targets to work toward. Students are thereby motivated and better able to understand the complexity of the learning process. When they are made aware that learning will not only include knowledge outcomes, but reasoning, problem solving, and various performance skills as well, they realize that memorizing material will not suffice. They must use various types of learning procedures and actively participate in the learning process to achieve the intended outcomes.

Instructional objectives also provide a basis for student self-assessment of learning progress. If students are to become independent learners, they must develop self-assessment skills. In writing, for example, students are encouraged to review and revise their written work before submitting it. This requires an understanding of the qualities of good writing, which are made clear in well-stated writing objectives. By sharing with students the intended outcomes of a performance or skill at the beginning of the instruction, we not only provide direction to their learning but we also provide them with a basis for evaluating their own progress and developing needed self-assessment skills.

Role of Objectives in Assessment

Well-stated instructional objectives make clear the type of performance to be assessed. They describe what students should know and be able to do as a result of learning. Assessment is then simply a matter of using an assessment instrument that best measures that particular type of performance. To assess a knowledge outcome, a paper-and-pencil test might do. But if it is a performance outcome (e.g., writing, speaking, psychomotor skill), some method of judging the performance skill or resulting product is required. Here, the instructional objectives help clarify the criteria to be used in judging the performance and the type of assessment technique needed.

Role of Objectives in Communicating Instructional Intent to Others

Instructional objectives that are stated as intended learning outcomes help clarify to parents and others how students will demonstrate that they have learned. Objectives also provide teachers with a basis for selecting samples of student work to share in parent–teacher conferences. Essentially, this process enables teachers to say this is what we are trying to do and this is how well we are doing it.

Role of Objectives in Evaluating Instruction

Clearly stated instructional objectives can illuminate the successes and failures in our instruction. This enables us to look for the reasons for failure in the methods, the materials, or the objectives themselves. In some cases we may need to change the methods and materials of instruction (e.g., use more complex material and student participation to develop reasoning skills). In others, the objectives may need to be modified or made clearer to students.

Focusing on Intended Learning Outcomes

There are, of course, many different ways of stating instructional objectives. One common type of statement is in terms of what we, as teachers, are going to do. Thus, we might have a statement like the following:

> To demonstrate to students how to set up laboratory equipment.

The difficulty with such a statement is that it focuses attention on the teaching activity rather than on the learning outcomes to be attained by the students. Literally speaking, we have achieved the objective once we have completed the demonstration—whether or not the students have learned anything from it. A more fruitful way to state instructional objectives is in terms of the outcomes we expect from our teaching; therefore, after we demonstrate how to use laboratory equipment, we might expect students to be able to do the following:

1. Identify the laboratory equipment used in the demonstration.
2. Describe the steps to be followed in setting up the laboratory equipment.
3. List the necessary precautions in handling and setting up the laboratory equipment.
4. Demonstrate skills in setting up their own laboratory equipment.

When instructional objectives are stated like this, they direct attention to the students and to the types of performance students are expected to exhibit as a result of the learning experience. Our focus thus shifts from the teacher to the students and from the learning *process* to the learning *outcomes*. This shift clarifies the intent of our instruction and provides the basis for an assessment of student learning.

The distinction between stating objectives in terms of what you are going to do as a teacher and stating them in terms of the learning outcomes you expect from your students is an important one. To check on your grasp of this distinction, look at the following two objectives and decide which one is stated as an expected learning outcome.[2]

1. Instills a comprehension of the scientific method.
2. Distinguishes between valid and invalid conclusions.

You should have selected the second objective, which clearly specifies how students will demonstrate at the end of the instructional period that they have learned. Note that the statement begins with a verb that implies an activity on the part of the student. There is no need to add such refinements as "The student has the ability to *distinguish*," "The student can *distinguish*," or "The student should be able to demonstrate that he or she can *distinguish*." The less wordy the objective, the better. Our aim is to indicate clearly the intent of our instruction in terms of the type of response (*distinguishes between*) that the student is expected to show.

The word *instills* in the first statement implies that the teacher, not the student, is engaging in an activity. By omitting this word, you can restate this objective in terms of a learning outcome as follows:

Comprehends the scientific method.

Note that although this objective is now stated as an outcome, the term *comprehends* is much more general than the term *distinguishes between*. To indicate clearly

---

[2]Throughout Part I you will be presented with opportunities for self-testing. To reap the most benefit, you should choose between alternatives before you continue your reading.

the intent of our instruction, it would be necessary to further define this objective by listing the specific types of student performance we are willing to accept as evidence of their comprehension (e.g., explains the procedures, describes the importance of controlling variables). This process of stating general objectives and then of further defining them in terms of specific statements has some advantage over the use of single statements of objectives, as we shall see shortly. First, however, let's see if we can further clarify the meaning of "instructional objectives as intended learning outcomes" by taking a look at their role in the instructional process.

Learning Outcomes and the Instructional Process

The relation of learning outcomes to the learning experiences provided during the teaching–learning phase of instruction is shown in the following diagram.

Student	→	TEACHING-LEARNING PROCESS	→	LEARNING OUTCOMES (End Products)
		Learning experiences based on interaction of subject matter, teaching methods, and instructional materials		Knowledge Comprehension Application Thinking skills Performance skills Computer skills Communication skills Computational skills Work-study skills Social skills Attitudes Interests Appreciation Adjustments

This diagram makes clear the fact that the learning experiences provided during the teaching–learning process are not ends in themselves but means to ends. The subject matter, the teaching methods, and the materials used in instruction are to be viewed as tools to bring about desired learning outcomes.

Although the diagram appears simple, the *process* of instruction and the *products* of instruction are frequently confused in statements of instructional objectives. For example, which of the following objectives is stated as a *product* (i.e., a learning *outcome*)?

1. Increases proficiency in the use of charts and graphs.
2. Interprets charts and graphs.

You are correct if you selected the second objective, which describes in general terms what the student does at the end of the learning experience. We later would want to clarify further what we mean by *interprets* (e.g., identifies a given point on a graph, describes the trend shown in a graph), but this instructional objective is definitely stated as a learning *product*.

In the first statement the term *increases* provides a clue that we are concerned with a *process*. The statement doesn't clarify how the student is to demonstrate increased proficiency at the end of the instruction. Is the student to interpret charts and graphs, to construct charts and graphs, or to give a speech in which charts and graphs will be used as visual aids? Stating objectives in terms of the learning *process* is misleading because one learning experience may contribute to many different learning outcomes, and one learning outcome (e.g., a scientific attitude) may be the result of many different learning experiences.

The first step in instructional planning, then, should be to identify and define our instructional objectives as learning outcomes. When we specify the types of performance (e.g., knowledge, understanding, skills) that we expect students to be able to demonstrate at the end of instruction, we can more wisely select the materials and methods of instruction. The statements of intended outcomes also clarify the specific types of performance to be tested when assessing student learning and can be used to convey our instructional intent to students, parents, and others who might be interested.

Stating Instructional Objectives as Intended Learning Outcomes

As noted earlier, objectives can be stated as learning outcomes in two ways. One is to list each specific type of performance students are to exhibit at the end of the instructional period. For example, we might start a list concerned with terminology as follows:

1. Defines the term in their own words.
2. Identifies the meaning of the term when used in context.
3. Distinguishes among terms that are similar in meaning.

A second method is to state the general instructional objectives and then to clarify each objective by listing a *sample* of the specific types of student performance we are willing to accept as evidence of the attainment of that objective. This procedure would result in statements such as the following:

1. Comprehends the meaning of terms.
    1.1. Defines the term in their own words.
    1.2. Identifies the meaning of the term when used in context.
    1.3. Distinguishes among terms that are similar in meaning.

Note that the specific statements are the same in both instances. The first list, however, implies that these types of performance are ends in themselves and that instruction is to be given directly in the specified performance. For example, we teach students "to define a term in their own words"; then, to test achievement of the outcome, we ask them "to define the term in their own words." This one-to-one relationship between the performance taught and the performance tested is characteristic of the training level and is widely used in programmed instruction. For regular classroom instruction, however, this procedure is useful only for teaching the simplest skills and the lowest levels of knowledge.

Stating the general instructional objective first and then clarifying it further by listing the specific types of performance that characterize that objective is more than a matter of literary form. This procedure makes clear that the instructional objective is *comprehension* and not *defining, identifying,* or *distinguishing among.* These latter terms simply describe a *sample of the types of performance that represent comprehension.* A different sample of specific types of performance could serve equally well. For example, we might use the following list instead of the one cited earlier.

1. Comprehends the meaning of terms.
    1.1. Relates terms to the concepts they represent.
    1.2. Uses each term in an original sentence.
    1.3. Identifies similarities and differences between terms.

Note that the instructional objective is still *comprehension.* We have merely listed a new sample of student performance to characterize what is meant by the statement "Comprehends the meaning of terms." It would be impossible to list all types of performance that might show comprehension; therefore, we must settle for a representative sample.

The particular sample of student performance that is selected to define an objective depends on both the level of the instruction and the nature of the content. The general objective "Comprehends the meaning of terms" could be an appropriate learning outcome at the elementary, secondary, or college level. However, at the elementary level the sample of performance might consist of specific statements such as "identifies pictures of the term" (e.g., largest) and "follows directions indicated by the term" (e.g., add these numbers); whereas, at the high school or college level such specific outcomes as "describes the concept the term represents" and "uses the term correctly in stating a principle" may be more appropriate. Similarly, the specific sample of performance can vary somewhat with the subject being taught. For example, English teachers may find that statements such as "defines the term in their own words" and "uses the term in an original sentence" best clarify their intended outcomes, whereas science teachers may favor such statements as "distinguishes among terms" and "describes the process represented by the term." Thus, teachers at all levels and in various subject-matter areas might use some of the same general objectives, such as "Comprehends the meaning of terms," but each may describe the student performance they are willing to accept as evidence of comprehension differently, depending on the level and nature of the instruction. Thus, it is the list of specific statements that describes the intended learning outcomes in terms of student performance. These are called *specific learning outcomes* (see Figure 1.2).

The fact that specific learning outcomes simply serve as *samples* of the types of performance we are willing to accept as evidence of the attainment of our general instructional objectives has implications for both teaching and assessment. Our teaching efforts must be directed toward the general objectives of instruction and not toward the specific samples of performance we have selected to represent each objective. For

Figure 1.2   Some Basic Terminology

General Instructional Objective	An intended outcome of instruction that has been stated in general enough terms to encompass a domain of student performance (e.g., "Comprehends the literal meaning of written material"). A general instructional objective must be further defined by a set of specific learning outcomes to clarify instructional intent.
Specific Learning Outcome	An intended outcome of instruction that has been stated in terms of specific and observable *student performance* (e.g., "Identifies details that are explicitly stated in a passage"). Specific learning outcomes describe the types of performance that learners will be able to exhibit when they have achieved a general instructional objective (specific learning outcomes are also called *specific objectives, performance objectives,* and *measurable objectives*).
Student Performance	Any measurable or observable student response that is a result of learning.

example, in teaching a *comprehension of terms*, we might have the students study the textbook definitions, compare and contrast the terms during class discussion, and use the terms in oral and written work. When we test the students, however, we present them with a list of terms and ask them to define each term in their own words and to write an original sentence using the term. Note that the test calls for a type of response that was not directly taught during classroom instruction. This is necessary if the test results are to show a *comprehension* rather than merely a *recall* of previous learning. Also, the test calls forth only a sample of the types of performance that might be used to represent a *comprehension of terms*. It would be impractical to include test items that measure all aspects of understanding, just as it would be impractical to include all relevant terms in a particular test. In both cases we must be satisfied with a *sample*—a sample of the many terms that the students have studied during instruction and a sample of the many types of performance that could be used as evidence of the student's comprehension of terms. If our samples are carefully chosen, we can generalize from our test results to the larger achievement domain. That is, we can estimate how well the students have achieved our instructional objective, the *comprehension of terms*.

Although it is the specific learning outcomes that specify the types of learning responses we are willing to accept as evidence of learning, the statements of general objectives provide several useful functions:

1. They make clear the variety of types of learning expected from the instruction (i.e., knowledge, comprehension, thinking skills, performance skills).
2. They provide a focus for instruction that avoids concentrating on isolated and unrelated learning tasks.
3. They are general enough to permit flexibility in choosing teaching methods and materials.

Figure 1.3   Why Not Include Conditions and Standards?

It is sometimes suggested that in addition to describing the desired *student performance*, an objective should include the *conditions* under which the performance is to be demonstrated and the *standard* of performance to be accepted. This method of stating objectives would result in a statement as follows (each element is identified to the left of the statement):

Condition	Given a drawing of a flower
Performance	the student will label in writing
Standard	at least 4 of the 5 parts shown.

Statements such as this are especially useful for programmed instruction and for mastery testing in simple training programs. When used for regular classroom instruction, however, they result in long, cumbersome lists that restrict the freedom of the teacher. If we restated the above as "Identifies the parts of a given plant structure," it could be used with various units of study and the teacher would be free to use real plants, pictures, diagrams, slides, or other stimulus material. Also, the students could respond orally, in writing, or simply by pointing to a named part. The standard (in this case 80%) could be set at the time of testing, either for the whole test or separately for each part. Keeping the standard separate from the objective makes it possible to vary the standards as needed without rewriting the objectives. For example, we may want to set lower standards at the beginning of a unit of study and higher standards at the end. Similarly we may want to set higher standards for a gifted group and lower standards for a group of students with mental retardation. Let's not waste time rewriting objectives to fit changing conditions.

4. They provide a framework for planning and preparing assessments and for interpreting assessment results.

What About Conditions and Standards?

The method of stating objectives described here doesn't include the *conditions* under which the performance is to be demonstrated nor the *standards* for determining a satisfying level of performance. Although conditions and standards may be useful for some simple skills and training programs, good reasons exist for not including them as part of classroom instructional objectives (See Figure 1.3). The relatively recent emphasis on intended learning outcomes that focus on solving "real-life" problems also stresses the need for more general standards than those tied to each specific learning outcome. This problem-solving approach typically requires describing standards of excellence in terms of a general procedure (e.g., planning a research study) or a general product (e.g., a written report). Assessment of the process or product uses scoring rubrics (i.e., scoring guidelines) that describe levels of excellence for the process or product as a whole. This approach will be discussed and illustrated in Chapter 11. It is mentioned here as one more reason for not including a standard with each instructional objective or specific learning outcome. For complex learning outcomes, broader statements of standards are needed to reflect the integrated nature of the instructional objective.

Summary

1. Instructional objectives are most useful for classroom instruction when stated as intended learning outcomes and defined in terms of student performance.

2. Instructional objectives, stated as intended learning outcomes, provide direction for instruction, guidelines for learning, targets for assessment, convey instructional intent to others, and provide for evaluation of instruction.

3. The two-step process of stating the general instructional objectives and further defining them with specific learning outcomes provides a focus for teaching, learning, and assessment without limiting the teacher's flexibility in selecting instructional methods and materials.

4. Although it may be possible to state all of the specific learning outcomes for simple learning tasks, as in a training program, for most classroom instruction only a sample of the specific learning outcomes can be stated for each objective.

5. The specific learning outcomes describe what types of student performance indicate that an objective has been achieved. Thus, common general objectives (e.g., Comprehends terms) can be adapted to various content areas and levels of instruction by writing specific learning outcomes that are relevant to the particular situation.

6. The conditions and standards of student performance should not be included in statements of objectives, but rather should be considered when student learning is assessed. This results in less cumbersome statements of objectives, provides greater flexibility in teaching, and permits the changing of conditions and standards to fit new situations without the need for rewriting objectives. It also permits the use of broader standards for complex learning outcomes (e.g., problem solving using realistic contextual settings).

Chapter 2

Obtaining Clear Statements of Instructional Objectives

After reading this chapter, you should be able to:

1. Distinguish between well-stated and poorly stated general instructional objectives.
2. Describe the procedure for defining general instructional objectives in performance terms.
3. Distinguish among verbs that indicate instructional intent and those that are merely learning indicators.
4. Write a set of instructional objectives for a unit or course of instruction.
5. Prepare a list of criteria for determining whether a set of instructional objectives is well stated.

As noted in the first chapter, objectives for most classroom learning should be stated in two steps: (1) stating the general instructional objectives as intended learning outcomes, and (2) defining each general instructional objective by listing a sample of the specific types of student performance that represents achievement of the objectives. The procedure sounds simple enough, but many teachers find it difficult at first. Here we shall describe and illustrate how to state instructional objectives that clearly convey instructional intent and provide an effective guide for teaching, learning and assessment.

Stating the General Instructional Objectives

If the general instructional objectives are to be clearly stated as intended learning outcomes, a number of errors must be avoided. One of the most common errors, mentioned earlier, is to describe teacher performance rather than student performance. Look at the following two objectives, for example, and note the difference in how they are stated. Which one most clearly indicates an instructional outcome?

1. Comprehends assigned reading material.
2. To increase the students' reading ability.

You should have had little difficulty selecting the first statement, which contains an expected outcome of instruction. Later we would need to list a sample of the specific types of performance that we are willing to accept as evidence that the student *comprehends*, but as stated this is a good general outcome.

The second statement offers a less clear picture of the intended results of instruction. It also gives the psychologically unsound impression that it is the teacher who is going to do the increasing rather than the student.

Another common error was also mentioned in Chapter 1; that is, stating an objective in terms of the learning *process* rather than as a learning *product*. The following two statements will clarify the difference. Which one is stated as a *product* of instruction, i.e., an instructional *outcome*?

1. Gains knowledge of basic principles.
2. Applies basic principles to new situations.

If you selected the second statement, you are correct. This statement clearly indicates what the student can do at the end of instruction. The first statement emphasizes the *gaining* of knowledge—the learning *process* rather than the type of performance that provides evidence that learning has taken place. Words like *gains*, *acquires*, and *develops* give away the fact that an objective is focused on the learning *process* rather than on the expected *outcome* of the learning experience.

In some cases in which objectives are stated in terms of the learning process, the instructional intent is still fairly clear. This is often true for simple learning outcomes. For example, in the statement "Develops skill in adding whole numbers," the learning outcome is obvious. In other cases, however, a single learning experience might contribute to any number of learning outcomes, none of which is apparent in the statement of objectives. For example, look at the following statement.

Learns symbols on a weather map.

This statement does clarify what the student is to learn, but it does not clarify the learning *outcomes* toward which the student should be directed. The teacher who wrote this statement might have in mind any one of the following learning outcomes:

Recalls the symbols used on a weather map.

Identifies the symbols on a weather map.

Interprets a weather map (using the symbols).

Constructs a weather map (using the symbols).

Predicts weather from a weather map (using the symbols).

The statement "learns symbols" obviously does not indicate the intent of the instruction as clearly as the statements of learning *outcomes* in the list. Identifying the nature of the desired product provides greater direction for planning, carrying out, and assessing the learning experiences.

Another common error in stating objectives is simply to list the subject matter to be covered. This error can be seen in a comparison of the following two statements. Which one is properly stated?

1. Principles of electricity.
2. Comprehends basic principles.

The correct answer is, of course, the second statement. The first statement is no more than a subject-matter topic. It contains no indication of what the students are expected to do with regard to the principles of electricity. Are they simply to know them, to comprehend them, or to apply them in some way?

The second statement could read "Comprehends principles of electricity," but there is some advantage in broadening the statement to include all types of principles covered in the instruction. The same outcome can then be used to indicate the expected reaction to any principle studied. When this is done, the specific types of student response used to clarify what is meant by the word *comprehends* must, of course, be *performance* oriented rather than *content* oriented. When complete, the statement of the objective and of the specific learning *outcomes* might appear as follows:

1. Comprehends basic principles.
    1.1. States the principle in his or her own words.
    1.2. Identifies an example of the principle.
    1.3. Distinguishes between correct and incorrect applications of the principle.
    1.4. Predicts an outcome based on the principle.

Note that the specific statements do not indicate what principles the students are to comprehend, but rather what *performance* they are to demonstrate as evidence that they comprehend. By not including a reference to subject matter in statements of learning outcomes, you can develop a set of outcomes that is useful with various units of instruction throughout a course. Thus the subject matter in each unit of instruction will indicate the principles that are to be studied, and the learning *outcomes* will indicate the types of reactions the students are to make to the principles.

Another common error is to include more than one type of learning *outcome* in each general objective. Look at the following two statements. Which one contains a *single outcome*?

1. Uses appropriate experimental procedures in solving problems.
2. Knows the scientific method and applies it effectively.

The first statement is correct; the second statement includes both *knows* and *applies* as possible *outcomes*. It is better to have a separate statement for each because some students may know the scientific method (i.e., be able to describe it) but may not be able to apply it effectively. With separate statements, you can define each objective in terms of specific learning outcomes and thus determine how well each objective is being achieved.

Figure 2.1   Stating Instructional Objectives

Observe the following precautions when stating instructional objectives:

1.   Don't state them in terms of *teacher performance*. (e.g., "Teach students scientific concepts.")

2.   Don't state them in terms of the *learning process*. (e.g., "Student learns scientific concepts.")

3.   Don't focus on the *subject-matter* topics. (e.g., "Student learns the meaning of osmosis, photosynthesis, etc.")

4.   Don't include two objectives in one statement. (e.g., "Student knows and comprehends scientific concepts.")

State and define each objective in terms of the type of *student performance* that is to be demonstrated at the end of instruction, as illustrated below:

1.   Comprehends scientific concepts.

   1.1.   Defines the concept.

   1.2.   Identifies an example of the concept.

   1.3.   States hypotheses based on the concept.

   1.4.   Describes how the process functions in a given situation.

   1.5.   Describes an experiment that illustrates the process.

In this section we have focused on some common errors to avoid in stating the general instructional objectives: stating the objectives in terms of (1) the teacher's performance, (2) the learning process, (3) the subject matter, and (4) a combination of two or more outcomes. These errors can be avoided by *focusing attention on the students and on the type of performance they are expected to demonstrate at the end of instruction*. Instructional objectives, then, should be brief, clear statements that describe instructional intent in terms of the desired learning *outcomes* (see Figure 2.1).

In addition to avoiding the common errors in stating instructional objectives, one of the most difficult tasks is to select the proper level of generality in stating each major objective.

Selecting the Proper Level of Generality

When developing a list of general instructional objectives for a course (or unit of course work), our aim is to create a list of outcomes to work toward and not a list of specific tasks to be performed by all students. To be sure, each general instructional objective will need to be defined further by a sample of the specific types of student performance that characterize each objective, but at this stage we are focusing only on the stating of the general objectives (see Figure 2.2).

Figure 2.2   Examples of General Instructional Objectives

Reading
1. Knows word meanings.
2. Comprehends the literal meaning of written material.
3. Infers meaning from written material.
4. Interprets tables, graphs, maps, and diagrams.
5. Evaluates written material using specific criteria (e.g., realistic, accurate).
6. Adapts reading rate to material and purpose of reading.
7. Locates information by using guides (e.g., index, table of contents, reference works).
8. Demonstrates a positive attitude toward reading.

Mathematics
1. Knows the meanings of terms and symbols.
2. Computes accurately and rapidly.
3. Comprehends mathematical concepts and processes.
4. Comprehends the number systems.
5. Applies concepts and processes to mathematical problems.
6. Invents new mathematical applications or generalizations.
7. Interprets measuring instruments, tables, and graphs.
8. Demonstrates a positive attitude toward mathematics.

Science
1. Knows the meaning of terms.
2. Knows specific facts.
3. Knows laboratory procedures.
4. Comprehends concepts and principles.
5. Applies concepts and principles to new situations.
6. Demonstrates skills and abilities needed to conduct an experiment.
7. Interprets data in scientific reports.
8. Displays a scientific attitude.

You may have noticed by now that each of the instructional objectives used in this chapter to illustrate properly stated learning outcomes began with a verb. The following verbs were used in these statements.

applies

comprehends

knows

uses

These verbs provide a clue to the desired level of generality for our major objectives. They are specific enough to provide direction for instruction without overly restricting the teacher or reducing the instruction to the training level. They are also specific enough to be easily defined by a brief list of the types of performance students are to demonstrate when the objectives have been achieved.

Let's look at a few statements that illustrate the problem of selecting a proper level of generality. Which one of the following statements represents the most general objective? Which one the most specific?

1. Communicates effectively in English.
2. Writes clear, effective English.
3. Punctuates sentences properly.

The first statement represents the most general objective. In fact, it is probably too general for a major objective because communication includes speaking, listening, writing, and reading. Each of these areas is general enough to provide a major objective by itself.

The most specific is the third statement, which might be a good specific learning outcome to be listed under a more general objective, but is probably too specific to be used as a general instructional objective. Thus the second statement comes closest to the desired level of generality. It clearly indicates the nature of the expected learning *outcome*, and it can be defined by a relatively short, clear list of specific learning outcomes.

Stating the Specific Learning Outcomes

After preparing a tentative list of general instructional objectives, you are ready to define each general objective in terms of the specific types of student performance that you are willing to accept as evidence that the objective has been achieved. These *specific learning outcomes* provide an operational definition of what we mean when we state that a student "knows terms", "comprehends principles", or "interprets charts and graphs". Unless the general objectives are further clarified in this way, they will not provide an adequate framework for teaching, student learning, or assessment.

The following general instructional objective and list of specific learning outcomes illustrates what is meant by defining instructional objectives in terms of *student performance*.

1. Knows specific facts (U.S. history)
    1.1. Identifies important dates, events, places, and people.
    1.2. Describes the characteristics of a given historical period.
    1.3. Lists important events in chronological order.
    1.4. Relates events to their most probable causes.

Note that each specific learning outcome starts with an *action verb* that indicates *observable* student responses; that is, responses that can be seen by an outside observer.

These verbs are listed as follows to clarify the types of terms needed for stating the specific learning outcomes.

identifies

describes

lists

relates

These verbs describe the types of responses the students are to exhibit as evidence that they have achieved the general instructional objective "Knows specific facts." As noted earlier, these responses provide only a sample of the specific outcomes that could be included under this objective. The list might be lengthened, shortened, or radically modified to fit the emphasis of a particular course. As an instructor you must define your own instructional objectives in terms of the specific learning outcomes you deem most appropriate. All we are doing here is illustrating the process of stating the specific outcomes in terms of identifiable student performance.

To check on your ability to distinguish between appropriate and inappropriate terms, look at the following two statements. Which one is stated in terms of student performance?

1. Realizes the importance of neatness.

2. Explains the importance of neatness.

You are correct if you selected the second statement. The term "explains" indicates a response that is definite and observable. The first statement does not specify how students will demonstrate that they *realize* the importance of neatness. Will they give reasons for being neat or will they dress more neatly? Terms such as this are subject to many interpretations and should be avoided when you state the specific learning outcomes for each general objective. Let's try another pair of statements to be sure you can tell the difference between *performance* and *nonperformance* terms. Which one of the following clearly indicates student performance?

1. Predicts the outcome of an experiment.

2. Sees the value of an experiment.

This time you should have had little difficulty in selecting the first statement as the correct answer. The term "sees" in the second statement is a common one in education (e.g., "I see the point"), and its familiarity might have misled you. But *sees* refers to an internal state. What will the students do when they see the value of an experiment? Will they describe its usefulness, point out its theoretical implications, or estimate the social consequences of the results? We simply can't tell because the term *sees* is vague, indefinite, and describes a reaction that is not directly observable.

In stating specific learning outcomes, then, it is wise to begin each statement with a verb that specifies definite, observable student performance. Such statements clarify from the outset the types of responses students are expected to make when they have achieved the general objective. Helpful lists of verbs for stating specific learning outcomes are included in Appendix C.

Obtaining a Representative Sample of Specific Learning Outcomes

When defining a general objective with a list of specific learning outcomes, you will need to decide how many specific outcomes to list for each objective. No hard-and-fast rules exist for this. Simple knowledge and skill outcomes obviously will require fewer specific outcomes than more complex ones, but even relatively simple instructional objectives may encompass such a large number of specific types of performance that only a portion of them can be listed. Take "knowledge of terms," for example, and note the various types of student performance that might be listed.

1. Knows the meaning of terms.
    1.1.   Writes a definition of the term.
    1.2.   Identifies a definition of the term.
    1.3.   Identifies the term that fits a given description.
    1.4.   Identifies a synonym of the term.
    1.5.   Identifies an antonym of the term.
    1.6.   Identifies an example of the term.
    1.7.   Identifies the term represented by a symbol (e.g., +, -).
    1.8.   Draws a picture that represents the term (e.g., circle, square).
    1.9.   Describes the procedure the term represents.
    1.10.   States the concept or principle that fits the term.
    1.11.   Describes the relationship of the term to a second term.
    1.12.   Differentiates between the term and a second term.
    1.13.   Differentiates between the technical meaning and the common meaning of the term.
    1.14.   Identifies the best meaning of the term when used in a sentence.
    1.15.   Distinguishes between proper and improper usage of the term.

This list is not exhaustive, making clear the futility of attempting to list all possible specific types of responses that represent a particular objective. All we can reasonably expect to do is list a sample of the specific types of performance that the students are expected to demonstrate when they have achieved the objective. The aim is to select as representative a sample as possible, so that students' performance on the selected outcomes will be characteristic of what their performance would be like on similar outcomes encompassed by the same general instructional objective. Typically, four to eight specific learning outcomes will be sufficient to describe an objective, but in some cases (e.g., a complex learning outcome) more outcomes may be needed.

The specific outcomes that best represent a general instructional objective will be modified by both the nature of the subject taught and the grade level at which the instruction is given. For "knowing terms," for example, a reading teacher would be likely to stress the identification of synonyms, antonyms, the meaning of words in context, and similar outcomes related to reading ability, whereas a math teacher would emphasize outcomes that relate the meaning of terms to symbols (e.g., x, =), figures (e.g., types of angles), operations (e.g., grouping into *sets*), and the like. Similarly, a primary teacher would be likely to state fewer and simpler types of outcomes based on picture identification and student drawings.

When the instructional objectives are *complex*, special care is needed to include all key elements. To identify the key elements in complex objectives, it is often necessary to consult reference books and other relevant materials. You are not likely to find a neat list of outcomes from which to choose, but even general discussions of the concepts will help to define the objectives. Thus, when objectives are concerned with *thinking skills*, *scientific inquiry*, and the like, a trip to the library might be needed.

Complex objectives are difficult to define but are usually more important from an educational standpoint. Don't overload your list of instructional objectives with simple learning outcomes merely because they are easy to define.

Emphasizing Instructional Intent

The *action verb* is the key element in stating the specific learning outcomes that define each general instructional objective. The selection of action verbs thus is a vital step in the preparation of a useful set of objectives. In general, we should select those verbs that (1) most clearly convey our instructional intent and (2) most precisely specify the student performance we are willing to accept as evidence that the general instructional objective has been achieved. Unfortunately, action verbs vary widely in their ability to meet both criteria.

Some verbs communicate instructional intent well but are less precise concerning the specific response to be observed. Other verbs clearly indicate the performance to be observed, but the indicated response does not satisfactorily convey the intent of the instruction. Let's look at a few examples. Which one of the following most clearly conveys instructional intent? Which one most precisely specifies the performance to be observed?

1. Identifies the parts on a diagram for an electrical circuit.
2. Labels the parts on a diagram for an electrical circuit.

If you selected the first statement as most clearly conveying instructional intent, you are correct. In this particular instance, the focus of our instruction would be on the *identification* of the parts and not the labeling of them. Although the term *labels* is more descriptive of the precise response the students are expected to make, labeling is not the intended learning outcome. We assume students already know how to label.

In this instance, we are simply using labeling as one way that identification might be shown. Identification might also be shown by pointing to, touching, drawing, circling, underlining, and so on. These *indicators* of the "ability to identify" clearly specify the student performance, but they do not always make clear the *intent* of the instruction. Given a choice between the two, it is wise to select the verb that best conveys instructional intent when stating specific learning outcomes.

Keeping the Specific Learning Outcomes Useful for Various Units of Study

The specific learning outcomes need to be specific enough to convey instructional intent but general enough to be used with various units of study. For example, the following statements represent specific learning tasks for a particular lesson.

1. Identifies the parts of the heart.
2. Describes the functions of the heart.

These specific tasks can best be converted into more general statements of specific learning outcomes as follows:

1. Identifies the parts of a given structure.
2. Describes the functions of a given structure.

Statements like these clearly describe what type of performance the students are to demonstrate, but the responses are not tied to a specific body part. In fact, the revised statements would be useful with any animal or plant structure being studied. The advantage of keeping the statements broader is, of course, that a set of objectives can then be used with various units of study. The subject-matter topics in each unit specify the content the student is to react to, and the specific learning outcomes describe the types of reactions to be made by the students.

To be sure you grasp this distinction, look at the following pair of learning outcomes and decide which one would be most useful with various units of study.

1. Lists the major battles of World War II in chronological order.
2. Lists historical events in chronological order.

The second one is a common learning outcome that can be used repeatedly in a history course. This statement also illustrates that sometimes all we need to do is substitute generalized content (e.g., historical events) for specific content (e.g., World War II). Thus, when we find ourselves listing specific tasks such as the following, we might simply combine them into a single statement like "Distinguishes among geometric shapes."

1. Distinguishes between a circle and a square.
2. Distinguishes between a square and a rectangle.
3. Distinguishes between a rectangle and a triangle.

There is nothing basically wrong with combining the student responses and specific course content. This approach is useful for brief units of work and is especially helpful to beginning teachers when planning lessons. Even here, however, it is better to define the objectives for a course of instruction in more general terms and use the statements as models or templates for stating the tasks for specific lessons. Thus, the generalized statement (e.g., "Identifies the parts of a given structure") provides guidelines for stating the more specific types of performance students are to demonstrate at the end of a particular lesson (e.g., "Identifies the parts of the heart," "Identifies the parts of a flower"). Experienced teachers find it easier to make this transition to specific lessons without rewriting the intended outcomes in more specific terms. Thus, whether they are teaching about animals or plants, they expect their students to identify the parts of any given structure being studied.

Making Sure the Specific Learning Outcomes Are Relevant

It goes without saying that each specific learning outcome should be relevant to the instructional objective it is defining, but this criterion constitutes another area of difficulty in listing the specific statements. Look at the following two statements, for example. Which one should be listed under the general goal "Comprehends scientific principles"?

1. Makes a prediction using the principle.
2. States the textbook definition of the principle.

Given a choice between these two, we would have to select the first. The second statement implies no more than the simple recall of information and therefore would be best classified as a *knowledge* outcome. The first statement goes beyond the recall of previously learned facts and asks the student to use the principle in a way that reflects a comprehension of its meaning.

Revising the General Objectives as Needed

During the process of defining the general instructional objectives, it may be necessary to modify the original list. In identifying the specific learning outcomes for the objectives, you may realize that some of them are too general and need to be subdivided. An objective on *problem solving* in arithmetic, for example, might better express instructional intent if it is broken down into *computational skill* and *solving story problems*. In defining other objectives, you might note that the specific learning outcomes overlap to such a degree that it is desirable to combine two statements into a single objective. Thus, "Applies scientific procedures" and "Plans simple experiments" might best be combined into a single objective such as "Uses the scientific method effectively." Because instructional objectives can be stated in many ways and at various levels of generality, considerable flexibility exists in the formulation of the statements. The listing of the specific learning outcomes thus provides a good opportunity for evaluating the original list of instructional objectives and for revising them as necessary. The ultimate aim, of course, is to derive a final list of general objectives and specific learning outcomes that most clearly indicates your instructional intent. (Use the checklist in Appendix A for evaluating your final list of objectives.)

Summary

1. State each general instructional objective as an *intended learning outcome* (i.e., in terms of students' terminal performance).

2. Begin each general objective with a verb that encompasses a domain of student performance (e.g., *knows, comprehends, applies*). Omit "The student is able to. . . . "

3. State each general objective so that it includes only one general learning outcome (e.g., not "Knows and comprehends. . . . ").

4. State each general objective in a manner that is useful with various units of study (e.g., "Knows the meaning of terms").

5. State each general objective so that it encompasses a readily definable domain of specific learning outcomes and is free from overlapping with other objectives.

6. List beneath each general instructional objective a set of specific learning outcomes that indicates the types of terminal performance the students can demonstrate when they have achieved the objective.

7. Begin each specific learning outcome with an action verb that specifies *observable performances* and indicates *instructional intent* (e.g., *identifies, describes*).

8. The set of specific learning outcomes for each instructional objective should be relevant, representative, and useful with various units of study.

9. When defining the general instructional objectives in terms of specific learning outcomes, revise and refine the original list of general objectives as needed.

10. Don't neglect complex objectives (e.g., thinking skills) simply because they are difficult to define in terms of specific learning outcomes. Consult reference materials for help.

Chapter 3

Getting Started in Preparing Instructional Objectives

After reading this chapter, you should be able to:

1. State the advantages of using a frame of reference when preparing objectives.
2. Describe the sources for locating lists of objectives developed by others.
3. List the factors to consider when evaluating the final list of objectives.
4. Describe the advantages of developing objectives cooperatively.
5. Write sample instructional objectives for a given category of intended learning outcomes.

Now that you are ready to focus on objectives that clearly convey the intended outcomes of instruction, let's take a look at the process of preparing a list of objectives for a given unit or course of instruction. How do you get started? What are some of the considerations? Where can you get ideas for objectives? How do you select and review objectives for the final list? In other words, how do you put it all together so that you can prepare an appropriate list of objectives for an instructional area.

Obtaining the Proper Orientation

In the past, teaching, learning, and assessment were guided by specific "behavioral" objectives. The intended learning outcomes typically consisted of long lists of specific tasks that were sequenced in hierarchical fashion from simple to complex. The lower-level knowledge and skills were to be mastered before proceeding to the more complex tasks. This step-by-step procedure, based on behavioral psychology, resulted in long lists of specific statements describing in detail what students could do when they had mastered the specific tasks of each lesson. All too frequently, this approach led to long, unmanageable lists of tasks with teachers focusing on the students' responses to the individual tasks rather than the integrated performance the tasks were intended to build toward. This, no doubt, contributed to teachers' overemphasis on knowledge and simple skill outcomes. These were the easiest to specify, to teach, and to test. The use of specific behavioral objectives is still favored in some schools. It is probably most useful for learning simple skills, for individualized instruction, and for training programs.

The influence of behavioral psychology is rapidly being replaced by cognitive psychology, which favors focusing on learning complex outcomes from the beginning. The contention is that thinking and reasoning can occur at all levels of learning if students are actively engaged in constructing meaning from their experiences. Instead of the sequential achievement of specific learning outcomes from simple to complex, more integrated learning is favored with emphasis on problem solving, reasoning, thinking skills, and other complex types of performance outcomes. This approach also favors the use of comprehensive tasks more like those in the "real world" (e.g., how to reduce water pollution). Obviously, with this approach to teaching, learning, and assessment, the objectives cannot be reduced to a list of simple tasks to be mastered but require statements focusing on the more complex learning outcomes (e.g., "Uses mathematical concepts in describing a problem"). The teaching and testing of specific tasks is being replaced by greater emphasis on holistic learning and performance assessment using "real-world" problems.

These two approaches to learning clearly require quite different statements of intended learning outcomes. The method of stating objectives being described in this book provides a middle ground, which is probably favored in most schools. It provides a method for stating the objectives as intended learning outcomes, it includes all types of instructional objectives ranging from simple to complex, it clarifies the types of student performance each objective represents, and the statements are not tied to any particular type of instruction. You are free to select any methods and materials that you deem to be most useful. In short, it clarifies the intended outcomes of instruction in performance terms, not the means of achieving the outcomes.

Using a Frame of Reference as a Guide

As you begin to write instructional objectives, you might find it helpful to refer to some frame of reference that clarifies the various types of learning outcomes to consider. This will provide greater assurance that important objectives are not overlooked and provide a guide for stating and organizing the objectives.

A simple framework like that in Figure 3.1 illustrates the wide array of learning outcomes that might be considered for any given instructional area. It makes clear that many desirable learning outcomes go beyond the simple knowledge and skill outcomes so often overemphasized in classroom instruction.

Much more detailed and highly structured is the *Taxonomy of Educational Objectives* developed by teachers, psychologists, and test experts. It provides an older, but still useful, comprehensive framework for identifying and writing instructional objectives.

Figure 3.1 Types of Learning Outcomes Common to Many Areas and Levels of Instruction

Lower-Level Cognitive Outcomes
  Knowledge
  Comprehension
  Application
	Recalling
	Translating
	Interpreting
	Estimating
	Comparing
	Classifying
	Applying

Higher-Level Thinking Skills
  Analysis
  Synthesis
  Evaluation
	Identifying
	Analyzing
	Inferring
	Relating
	Formulating
	Generating
	Judging

Affective Outcomes
  Attitudes
  Interests
  Appreciations
  Adjustments
	Listening
	Responding
	Participating
	Seeking
	Demonstrating
	Relating
	Valuing

Performance Outcomes
  Procedure
  Product
  Procedure and product
  Problem solving
	Speaking
	Singing
	Drawing
	Computing
	Writing
	Contructing
	Demonstrating
	Operating
	Performing
	Originating

Taxonomy of Educational Objectives

The developers of *Taxonomy of Educational Objectives* attempted to identify all possible educational outcomes and classify them by general and specific categories, in a hierarchical pattern, somewhat like the classification of plants and animals.

The developers of the *Taxonomy* identified three domains of the educational outcomes: cognitive, affective, and psychomotor.[1]

---

[1] See Appendix B for detailed descriptions of the three domains and complete references to them.

1. *Cognitive:* Concerned with intellectual outcomes; the classification system ranges from lower-level knowledge outcomes to higher-level intellectual abilities and skills (Bloom, Englehard, Furst, Hill, & Krathwohl, 1956).

2. *Affective:* Concerned with outcomes in the areas of interests, attitudes, appreciation, and methods of adjustment, using a classification system ranging from receiving stimuli to developing a characteristic set of values that directs behavior (Krathwohl, Bloom, & Masia, 1964).

3. *Psychomotor:* Concerned with motor skills; one classification system (Simpson, 1972) ranges from perception of cues to origination of a new movement pattern.

The originators of the *Taxonomy* developed a complete classification system for the cognitive and affective domains but did not complete the psychomotor domain system as scheduled. Other individuals, however, not connected with the original taxonomy developers, have prepared at least two major classification systems for the psychomotor domain (Harrow, 1972; Simpson, 1972). We selected Simpson's for our use so that all three domains of the taxonomy could be presented.

The categories and subcategories in each of the three domains are arranged in hierarchical order, from the simplest outcomes to the most complex. (This arrangement required the use of new terminology that is sometimes confusing when first encountered; however, to obtain a classification system with a distinctive set of hierarchical categories, some of the more broadly defined traditional terminology had to be replaced with more clearly defined, limited terminology.) The cognitive domain, for example, includes the categories of knowledge, comprehension, application, analysis, synthesis, and evaluation. Note that the categories of the cognitive domain do not use such traditional terminology as *understanding* and *thinking* because these terms cut across categories. For example, understanding can be shown by performance at the comprehension or the application level. High-level thinking skills are covered by the top several levels of the cognitive domain.

The affective domain includes the categories of receiving, responding, valuing, organization, and characterization by a value or value complex. The traditional categories of interest, attitude, appreciation, and modes of adjustment overlap several of these taxonomy categories. Similarly, the psychomotor domain uses a set of categories ranging from simple to complex and the typical motor skills overlap several categories depending on the student's stage of development.

The three domains of the taxonomy provide a comprehensive and clearly structured classification system that provides a good frame of reference for preparing instructional objectives. But don't feel you must use the terminology of the taxonomy categories when writing objectives. You can state objectives in many ways, and how you state them is determined somewhat by the nature of the subject or skill area.

Also, while the three domains provide a discrete classification system, learning outcomes frequently overlap two or more domains. For example, cognitive outcomes have some affective components and motor skills typically include both cognitive and affective elements. Thus, rather than attempting to match the taxonomy categories slavishly, use the three domains to (1) get ideas for types of objectives to consider, (2) assist in obtaining clear statements and in arranging the list, and (3) check on the completeness of the final set of objectives.

Useful summaries of the main categories in the three domains are presented in Appendix B. Each category is briefly described and illustrated with lists of sample objectives and verbs for stating specific learning outcomes. The original references from which the summaries were derived are also included for those who wish to study the taxonomy in more detail. It might be useful to review the taxonomy descriptions in Appendix B at this point, or at least before embarking on the writing of objectives.

Alternative Frames of Reference

A number of other frames of reference have been suggested for classifying intended learning outcomes. Although these are not considered to be complete taxonomies, they do provide major categories to consider when compiling a list of instructional objectives.

A set of five major categories has been suggested by Gagné (1985). These categories cover the three broad areas of cognitive, affective, and psychomotor outcomes but emphasize the cognitive area. His list includes the following major categories:

1. *Verbal Information:* Concerned with the ability to declare or state verbal information. Can range from isolated facts to a network of interconnected ideas.

2. *Intellectual Skills:* Concerned with discriminations, concepts, rules, and procedures Can range from single and complete learning to complex and gradual learning.

3. *Cognitive Strategies:* Concerned with knowing where and how to use information and skills in learning and problem solving. Strategies can range from simple to complex.

4. *Motor Skills:* Concerned with physical movements that are gradually learned. Can range from simple (e.g., tying shoe laces) to complex (e.g., playing a piano).

5. *Attitudes:* Concerned with internal states that are inferred from external behavior. Can range from a simple positive or negative response to more complex behavior patterns.

These five types of learning differ both in the nature of the learning process and in the types of learning outcomes that result from the instruction. Thus, they provide a relatively simple framework for identifying and writing instructional objectives that include a variety of types of intended learning outcomes.

Another relatively simple framework for preparing instructional objectives was developed by Quellmalz (1985), although her list was limited to cognitive outcomes. This classification system includes the following categories:

1. *Recall:* Concerned with verbatim statements or recognition of information, ranging from simple facts to paraphrased information.

2. *Analysis:* Concerned with breaking down material into its component parts, ranging from simple to complex types of analyses.

3. *Comparison:* Concerned with comparing similarities and differences, ranging from simple to complex comparisons.

4. *Inference:* Concerned with deductive and inductive reasoning, ranging from simple to complex tasks.

5. *Evaluation:* Concerned with value judgments supported by evidence or relevant arguments, based on definite criteria, ranging from simple to complex judgments.

This classification system attempts to identify relatively discrete categories that increase in complexity. It is similar to the cognitive domain of the *Taxonomy of Educational Objectives,* but greatly simplified. As students move through the categories, from recall to evaluation, a higher level of performance is expected. The difficulty of the performance within categories is determined by the complexity of the task. For example, an elementary student might be required to evaluate a short story while a high school or college student might be asked to evaluate a novel. Thus, frameworks like this provide an easy-to-use classification system that can be adapted to all levels of instruction.

Cautions in Using Any Framework as a Guide

The various frames of reference provide useful guides for identifying and writing instructional objectives. They help obtain a more comprehensive and well-balanced list of intended learning outcomes. However, don't blindly follow any classification system. There is no need to develop objectives in an area just because it is listed in some framework. The nature of the course, the goals of the school program, and the curriculum guide will more likely shape your final list of objectives. Use the various classification systems in a creative way—to get ideas, to expand your list of outcomes, and to organize your objectives in some meaningful manner.

Other Guides in Preparing Instructional Objectives

You can use a number of sources for identifying, writing, and organizing objectives in a given area of instruction. Some states provide statewide objectives that serve as a basis for the goals and objectives included in curriculum guides at the local school level. In such states, it is important, of course, that your instructional objectives be in harmony with the statewide objectives reflected in the curriculum guides.

Curriculum Guides

Some libraries keep files of curriculum guides for teachers in training. You might find it useful to review a number of different guides, if they are available, to note the variation in coverage and the way the objectives are stated. If you are already teaching, or know where you will be teaching, you, of course, will want to consult any curriculum guide available.

Books and Special Reports

Many books on methods of teaching discuss objectives, present illustrative lists, and contain references that will help you locate others. The yearbooks and other references published by the National Council of Teachers of English, the National Council of Teachers of Mathematics, the National Council for the Social Studies, and the National Science Teachers Association also contain suggested lists of objectives from time to time. The more recent publications will give greater emphasis to the thinking–problem solving type of curriculum and the method of stating the intended learning outcomes will reflect this emphasis.

Textbooks and instructional materials at the elementary level typically contain lists of objectives for each lesson. However, they tend to focus on limited and detailed elements of content and are not always stated in performance terms (e.g., "Understand that living things need water"). These lesson-plan type of objectives can serve as a source of ideas for preparing instructional objectives for an area of instruction, if broadened (e.g., "Comprehends the elements needed to sustain life") and defined in performance terms (e.g., "Identifies the elements needed," "Explains the role of each element," "Describes what happens when there is a shortage of a particular element"). Objectives and specific learning outcomes such as these are more useful for planning both the instruction and the assessment of intended learning outcomes, and can also serve as a guide for more detailed statements for lesson plans.

An especially helpful guide is the *Encyclopedia of Educational Research*, which summarizes educational research on various topics. To use this reference, simply consult the section on the teaching of the particular subject in which you are interested. There you typically will find references to journal articles that contain information concerning objectives in your teaching area.

Test Manuals

Some recent achievement test batteries focus on curriculum standards in the various subjects suggested by the National Councils, discussed earlier, and by various commissions and curriculum projects. The test manuals, or separate publications, typically include statements of the learning outcomes being assessed, and thus provide another source of ideas for identifying and stating instructional objectives in your area of teaching. Emphasis in some of these recent achievement test manuals is on thinking, problem solving, and the use of realistic situations. Just remember that the intended learning outcomes stressed in achievement test batteries are those common to many schools nationwide, and therefore may not include those unique to a local instructional program.

Considerations in Selecting Instructional Objectives

It is usually possible to identify many more instructional objectives than can be achieved in a particular course or instructional unit. The constraints of time, teaching resources, and prerequisites to the instruction limit what we can expect students to learn. Thus these and other factors must be considered in compiling the final list. The following questions will serve as criteria for reviewing and selecting the most appropriate objectives to be included. They can also be a guide for an ongoing review of objectives during instruction to make sure that they remain in harmony with teaching and assessment.

Do the Objectives Indicate Learning Outcomes that Are Appropriate to the Instructional Area?

This question has no simple answers, but it has to be considered. Here we must turn to the recommendations of experts in the curriculum area in which you plan to teach. What learning outcomes do they consider to be most important? There will not be complete agreement here, but a review of their recommendations will help you identify the objectives that have the support of most curriculum specialists. This review will prevent any serious omissions and will provide greater assurance that your final list of objectives is in harmony with the most recent developments in the area.

Do the Objectives Represent All Logical Learning Outcomes of the Instructional Area?

Here we are concerned with the comprehensiveness and representativeness of the list of objectives. For example, are objectives included from all three areas of learning—cognitive, affective, and psychomotor? Does a proper balance exist among the three areas and within each area? Teachers in areas where intellectual skills are dominant have a tendency to overemphasize knowledge of specific facts and to neglect complex intellectual outcomes, attitudes, interests, and skills. On the other hand, teachers in areas where performance skills are dominant (art, music, physical education) often neglect the cognitive outcomes to be achieved.

Are the Objectives Attainable by These Particular Students?

To answer this question, we need to consider the prior achievement of the students and their cultural background. Are the students alike in terms of past achievement. Are some or all of the students from culturally disadvantaged homes? The nature of the student group and their readiness for particular learning experiences are important considerations in formulating and selecting objectives. Closely related concerns are the time allowed for the instruction and the facilities and teaching materials available. The development of thinking skills and changes in attitude, for example, are extremely time consuming because it depends on the cumulative effect of a long series of learning experiences. Similarly, some outcomes (e.g., skill in the scientific method) may require special laboratory facilities and teaching materials. We are not suggesting that otherwise desirable objectives be discarded, but simply that they may need to be modified to fit the student group and the instructional conditions under which they are to be achieved.

Are the Objectives in Harmony with the Philosophy of the School in Which the Instruction Is to Be Given?

This would be an easy criterion to apply if each school had a clear statement of philosophy or a list of educational objectives to serve as a guide. Unfortunately, many schools do not; you must infer which outcomes are most valued in such schools. If a school appears to emphasize independent work, self-discipline, freedom to explore new areas, and the democratic planning of activities, for example, these emphases should be reflected in the final list of instructional objectives. Similarly, if every teacher is expected to stress effective oral and written communication, thinking skills, and complex performance tasks, a broader range of instructional objectives will need to be included than might otherwise be the case. In short, your instructional objectives should be in harmony with the stated or implicit objectives of the total school program.

Are the Objectives in Harmony with Basic Principles of Learning?

As we indicated earlier, our instructional objectives should be stated as desired learning outcomes. Therefore, it is legitimate to ask to what extent our objectives are in harmony with what is known about the principles of learning. Some of the basic factors that should be considered are the following:

1. *Readiness:* Are the students mature enough to attain these particular objectives? Do the students have the necessary experiences and educational background to proceed successfully? Is there another level at which some of the objectives might be attained more readily?

2. *Motivation:* Do these objectives reflect the needs and interests of the students? Can they be restated or modified to be more closely related to the students' concerns? Is there another stage of development where these objectives would more closely fit the students' emerging interests?

3. *Retention:* Do these objectives reflect learning outcomes that tend to be retained longest (e.g., comprehension, application, thinking skills)? Are there other objectives that might be more lasting and that should be included?

4. *Transfer Value:* Do these objectives reflect learning outcomes that are widely applicable to new situations? Do the objectives include methods of study and modes of thinking that are most likely to contribute to future learning in the area? Do the objectives reflect realistic and complex learning tasks that are most useful in the "real" world?

These questions are not always easily answered, but they highlight the importance of considering the learning process when you formulate and select instructional objectives. Most general textbooks on educational psychology will provide extended discussions of the basic learning principles. It is sufficient to point out here that the more complex learning outcomes tend to be retained longer and to have greater transfer value. When they are appropriate to the developmental level of the learner, the more complex outcomes also have the greatest potential for arousing and maintaining student interest.

Preparing Instructional Objectives Cooperatively

It is desirable to have teachers prepare lists of instructional objectives cooperatively, wherever possible. This might involve teachers at the same grade level or in the same department working together, or it might involve committees of teachers representing all grade levels and all departments in the school. The cooperative development of objectives will ease the burden because the work can be divided among the teachers. In addition, this procedure provides greater assurance that (1) teachers of the same course are emphasizing the same learning outcomes, (2) the sequence of instructional objectives from one grade level to the next or one course to the next is appropriate, (3) a minimum of overlap exists in single-course objectives (e.g., knowledge of facts), and (4) proper attention is given to multiple-course objectives (e.g., library skills) in each teacher's lists.

Summary

1. Obtaining a proper orientation is important as an overall guide when preparing instructional objectives. In recent years, the focus has shifted to a curriculum that stresses thinking and problem solving in realistic contextual settings. The method of stating objectives described and illustrated in this book is readily usable with this approach, but it also can be used in more traditional learning programs.

2. A frame of reference that classifies the various types of learning outcomes can aid in identifying, stating, and organizing objectives into an appropriate list. It is especially useful in clarifying the broad range of complex learning outcomes that should be considered.

3. The *Taxonomy of Educational Objectives* is an older framework but it provides the most comprehensive and complete classification of cognitive, affective, and psychomotor objectives.

4. Other, simpler systems of classifying learning outcomes are available as guides for writing instructional objectives. These also include learning outcomes ranging from simple to complex, and, although less complete than the *Taxonomy*, they are easier to use.

5. Aid in preparing a list of objectives for an instructional area can also be obtained by consulting lists of objectives prepared by others. These can be found in curriculum guides, methods books, the publications of the National Councils in each subject area, and achievement test manuals.

6. Check your final list of instructional objectives for appropriateness, representativeness, attainability, relevance to the institutions instructional program, and relevance to the basic principles of learning.

7. In school settings, prepare instructional objectives cooperatively with other teachers, to assure uniformity within grade levels and proper sequencing between grade levels.

PART II

Writing Instructional Objectives for Various Outcomes

Chapter 4

Writing Objectives for Knowledge, Comprehension, and Application Outcomes

After reading this chapter, you should be able to:

1. Describe the characteristics of learning outcomes at the knowledge, comprehension, and application levels.
2. Write illustrative general instructional objectives for each of the three categories of objectives.
3. Write sample general objectives and specific learning outcomes to illustrate how objectives can be adapted to different *areas* of instruction.
4. Write sample general objectives and specific learning outcomes to illustrate how objectives can be adapted to different *levels* of instruction.
5. Write different versions of the same instructional objectives for some intended learning outcome.

Although the major emphasis is on thinking, problem solving, and other complex learning outcomes in education, learning programs are still concerned with objectives at the knowledge, comprehension, and application levels.

Knowledge outcomes are the lowest level of intellectual outcomes and are concerned with the recall or recognition of learned material. Comprehension is concerned with grasping the meaning of material as shown by interpretation, translation, prediction, and similar responses. Application is the ability to use the material in new situations. All three levels may be concerned with terms, facts, rules, procedures, concepts, principles, or theories.

Most content areas and levels of instruction include some emphasis on intended learning outcomes at the knowledge, comprehension, and application levels. In some cases these terms can be used directly in the statements of general instructional objectives, as shown in Figure 4.1.

In others, the statements may fit the instruction more closely if different terminology is used and the categories are simply used as a general framework. The following example illustrates this at the elementary level of instruction.

1. Distinguishes among geometric shapes (Knowledge).
    1.1 Draws a given shape (e.g., circle, square).
    1.2 Selects an object representing a given shape (e.g., ball, box).
    1.3 Identifies shapes of objects in a picture (e.g., building, lake).
    1.4 Describes objects using the names of shapes.
2. Interprets graphs (Comprehension).
    2.1 Identifies the value of a given position on a graph.
    2.2 Identifies the relative values of two given positions on a graph.
    2.3 Describes the trend indicated by a graph.
    2.4 Distinguishes between statements that are supported and unsupported by a graph.
3. Solves word problems (Application).
    3.1 Selects the proper procedure.
    3.2 Estimates the approximate result.
    3.3 Calculates the answer and compares with approximation.
    3.4 Checks the answer using another method.

There are many ways to state a general instructional objective and the specific learning outcomes clarify the types of student performance that represent achievement of the objective.

Stating Objectives at the Knowledge, Comprehension, and Application Levels

The level of learning expected increases as we go from knowledge to comprehension to application. The following objectives for a common outcome, the learning of terms, illustrates how the specific learning outcomes clarify the types of performance that characterize each level.

1. Knows common terms.
    1.1 Identifies a definition of the term.
    1.2 Identifies an example of the term.

Figure 4.1 Sample General
Instructional Objectives

Examples of knowledge, comprehension, and application outcomes in various content areas.

Mathematics
　　Knows the meaning of terms and symbols.
　　Comprehends mathematics concepts and processes.
　　Applies concepts and processes to mathematical problems.

Reading
　　Knows word meanings.
　　Comprehends the literal meaning of written material.
　　Applies reading skills to textbook material.

Writing
　　Knows the mechanics of writing.
　　Comprehends grammatical rules of writing.
　　Applies writing skills in laboratory reports.

Science
　　Knows scientific terms.
　　Comprehends scientific concepts and principles.
　　Applies concepts and principles.

Social Studies
　　Knows facts about social problems.
　　Comprehends effects of social problems on society.
　　Applies problem solving approach to social problems.

　　1.3 Writes a synonym of the term.

　　1.4 Writes an antonym of the term.

2. Comprehends the meaning of terms.

　　2.1 Defines a term in own words.

　　2.2 Distinguishes between correct and incorrect use of a term.

　　2.3 Explains the meaning of a term in light of its contextual setting.

　　2.4 Describes the similarities and differences of two terms similar in meaning.

3. Applies terms in written work.

　　3.1 Selects the term that best describes an idea, action, or event.

　　3.2 Writes a sentence using a given term.

　　3.3 Writes a paragraph using a given set of terms.

　　3.4 Uses new terms in assigned writing projects.

Describing the intended learning outcomes at each level makes it possible to identify students who know the material (e.g., by memorizing) but don't understand it well
enough to put it in their own words, identify examples of it, or apply it in some way.

In some cases the general objectives can be defined by specific learning outcomes that are useful in different areas of instruction and at several levels of instruction, as shown in our illustrative list. More commonly, however, the list of specific learning outcomes needs to be modified to reflect the specific types of performance expected from the instruction.

Adapting Statements to Areas of Instruction

Although it is desirable in stating and defining instructional objectives to keep the statements general enough to be useful with various units of study, they should be closely adapted to the instructional area. For example in writing specific learning outcomes for "Knows common terms" in mathematics, the following list of specific learning outcomes might be used.

1. Knows common terms (Math).
    1.1 Identifies the symbol that represents the term.
    1.2 Describes the procedure indicated by the term.
    1.3 Names the parts of a given problem.
    1.4 Writes a formula that represents the term.

Similarly, comprehension objectives in different subjects might be adapted as follows:

1. Comprehends Science Principles
    1.1 Identifies the principle in restated form.
    1.2 Describes examples of the principle.
    1.3 States hypotheses that are in harmony with the principle.
    1.4 Distinguishes between correct and incorrect interpretations of the principle.
2. Comprehends mathematics principles and procedures.
    2.1 Writes mathematical formulas from given verbal statements.
    2.2 Explains why a given procedure is selected to solve a particular problem.
    2.3 Describes a method for checking answers.
    2.4 States the principle on which a given operation is based.

Learning outcomes at the comprehension and application levels seem most appropriate for such content areas as science, mathematics, and social studies but less useful in courses emphasizing simple performance skills. A course like typing, for example, stresses primarily knowledge and skill outcomes, and there is little value in attempting to force the outcomes into the more complex categories of comprehension and application. Typing is an application of skill but this type of application is not the same as the "application" category we have been describing. The latter refers to the use of principles to solve problems that are new to the students. Thus it represents a higher level of understanding than comprehension, and does not refer to the application of performance skills as in typing.

Knowledge and skill play a major role in several areas. For example, at the elementary level, such areas as speaking, spelling, and simple computation skills would fall in this category. At the secondary level such courses as art, music, vocational courses, and physical education might include complex learning outcomes in some areas, but also have some that place major emphasis on knowledge and skill. Stating outcomes in the area of performance skills will be described in a later chapter. The main point is don't attempt to use the categories of *knowledge, comprehension* and *application* if they don't apply. In teaching how to play basketball, for example, don't use objectives like "Comprehends the rules of play" and "Applies the rules of play during a game." This implies a higher level of cognitive outcomes than the activity warrants. It is much better to state these outcomes as follows:

> Knows the rules of play.
>
> Follows the rules during a game.

Statements such as these indicate what the students are expected to be able to do, without implying there is some higher level of cognitive outcome involved. This illustrates why one should not become a slave to any particular classification system. Forcing statements of objectives to fit a certain set of categories has no advantage. The categories of knowledge, comprehension, and application should simply be guides for identifying possible objectives for a given area of instruction.

Adapting Statements to Levels of Instruction

Many intended learning outcomes are applicable to various levels of instruction. Common general instructional objectives that cut across grade levels can be adapted to a particular instructional level by means of the specific learning outcomes. For example, the objective "Knows basic concepts" might vary from the lower primary level to the upper secondary levels (high school and college) as follows:

1. Knows basic concepts (Lower Primary Level).
    1.1 Identifies a picture indicating relative position (e.g., first, last).
    1.2 Identifies a picture indicating relative size (e.g., biggest, smallest).
    1.3 Identifies a picture indicating relative amount (e.g., most, least).
    1.4 Identifies a picture indicating relative distance (e.g., farthest, nearest).
2. Knows basic concepts (Upper Secondary Level).
    2.1 Describes the characteristics of the concept.
    2.2 Identifies the concept from a brief description of it.
    2.3 Identifies symbols representing the concept.
    2.4 Distinguishes between the concept and similar concepts.

At the lower primary level the type of performance accepted as evidence of achievement of the objective must, of course, be stated in simpler and more specific terms. However, as illustrated here, if carefully stated, they can clearly convey what primary students can do to demonstrate that they know basic concepts.

These examples, showing how the same instructional objectives can be used at different levels of instruction by adapting them through the specific learning outcomes, does not imply that it is always wise to do so. It is probably most useful where there is an attempt to focus on those common objectives in the areas of basic concepts and skills that are emphasized throughout the various grade levels. Even then, it is often advantageous to modify a general instructional objective to more closely fit the emphasis at a particular level of instruction and merely classify the objective as a knowledge outcome.

As with knowledge outcomes, comprehension and application objectives can be adapted to the level of instruction by means of the specific learning outcomes. For example, comprehension of a short story at the lower primary level and the secondary level might vary as follows:

1. Comprehends a short story (Lower Primary Level).

    1.1 Describes what happened in the story.

    1.2 Chooses the most appropriate title for the story.

    1.3 Explains why the title is most appropriate.

    1.4 Explains why a particular event occurred in the story.

    1.5 Explains why the characters of the story acted as they did.

2. Comprehends a short story (Secondary Level).

    2.1 Describes the main theme of the story.

    2.2 Explains the significance of certain events in the story.

    2.3 Identifies similarities and differences between characters.

    2.4 States possible motivations for the actions of the characters.

    2.5 Describes what might happen next if the story were to be continued.

As noted earlier, there is no reason that comprehension outcomes must include the term *comprehension* in the statements of the general objectives. When writing objectives at the comprehension and application levels, you may want to use terminology that fits the subject more closely and describes student performance in more specific terms, as follows:

1. Translates from verbal to mathematical form (Comprehension).

    1.1 Converts words to numerals.

    1.2 Converts words to mathematical symbols.

    1.3 Converts verbal statements to mathematical formulas.

    1.4 Writes an equation that represents a word problem.

2. Writes a well-organized paragraph (Application).

    2.1 States a main idea.

    2.2 Relates sentences to the main idea.

2.3 Uses complete sentences.

2.4 Uses descriptive words to emphasize points.

2.5 Arranges sentences in a meaningful sequence.

2.6 Uses capitals and punctuation correctly.

2.7 Spells words correctly.

2.8 Maintains correct grammatical usage.

You can see from these examples that intended learning outcomes can be stated in various ways. The task is to state each general instructional objective and set of specific learning outcomes so that they most clearly describe student performance when the objectives have been achieved. Although knowledge, comprehension, and application outcomes are common to many areas of instruction, the outcomes must typically be adapted to a particular situation by variation in wording. Just be sure that the terminology selected is relevant to the area and level of instruction.

The Problem of Limiting Objectives to Intellectual Outcomes

Although we are focusing here on intellectual outcomes, it must be recognized that concomitant affective or psychomotor elements are often present as well. Our earlier objective "Comprehends a short story," for example, focused on intellectual reactions to the story, but students also may have emotional reactions to the story. Did the story change how students felt toward the people or events in the story? Did the students empathize with some of the characters? Did the students feel elated or bored by the story? These and similar questions may suggest outcomes that are equally important in assessing students' reactions to short stories. Such outcomes can be stated separately or incorporated as part of a larger objective that includes both comprehension and affect, depending on the nature of the instruction.

Similarly, psychomotor activities focus on skills but typically include both cognitive and affective components. Even such a routine skill as setting up laboratory equipment requires knowledge about the equipment, skill in selecting and assembling it, and an attitude of care during the procedure. Whether these are listed as separate objectives or combined to reflect the integrated nature of the activity, again, depends on the nature of the instruction. Use separate objectives if they more clearly convey the intended learning outcomes, but don't separate them just so they can be classified as cognitive, affective, or psychomotor.

Summary

1. Most areas of instruction include knowledge outcomes (i.e., remembering material), comprehension outcomes (i.e., grasping the meaning of material), and application outcomes (i.e., using the information in some way).

2. All three levels may be concerned with terms, facts, rules, procedures, concepts, principles, or theories, but the higher levels—comprehension and application— require the use of some novelty (e.g., new interpretations, new problems, new contextual settings).

3. The terms *knowledge, comprehension,* and *application* can be used directly in the statements of general objectives, if they are appropriate to the instruction and can be defined by a list of specific learning outcomes that clarifies their meaning.

4. In some cases the categories of knowledge, comprehension, and application simply provide a framework that serves as a guide for identifying objectives, that are then stated in more specific terms to fit a particular situation.

5. Some instructional objectives can be used for various areas and levels of instruction (e.g., "Knows basic terms") by writing specific learning outcomes that are relevant to each particular situation.

6. Some instructional objectives can best be adapted to a particular area or level of instruction by restating both the general instructional objectives and the specific learning outcomes.

7. Avoid stating objectives at the higher cognitive levels, if the intended learning outcomes require only knowledge and skills (e.g., typing).

8. It is usually better to state cognitive, affective, and psychomotor outcomes separately, but if an intended learning outcome is most clearly stated by including more than one type of performance in the objective, don't modify it simply so that the objectives can be classified into separate categories.

Chapter 5

Writing Objectives for Higher-Level Thinking Skills

After reading this chapter, you should be able to:

1. Describe the characteristics of thinking skills at the analysis, synthesis, and evaluation levels.

2. Distinguish between well-stated and poorly stated objectives at the thinking level.

3. Write a thinking skill objective and set of specific learning outcomes that are useful with various units of study.

4. Write a thinking skill objective and set of specific learning outcomes for a particular area and level of instruction.

5. Write a general instructional objective and set of specific learning outcomes that include both cognitive and affective outcomes at the thinking level.

Thinking skills and strategies have been described in many different ways. Such terms as *critical thinking, creative thinking,* and *problem solving* are commonly used frameworks for classifying specific sets of thinking skills and strategies. Critical thinking skills emphasize analysis and evaluation (e.g., identifying and analyzing a problem and evaluating possible solutions). Creative thinking skills emphasize the production of something new (e.g., producing a plan for solving a problem). Although critical and creative thinking are frequently described separately in the literature, elements of both are usually involved in various types of problem solving. Thus in this chapter we shall be concerned with thinking skills in general and not limit them to a particular type of thinking.

Thinking strategies in problem solving typically include a sequence of activities such as (1) identifying and analyzing a problem, (2) applying past learning, (3) gathering new information, (4) organizing and comparing data, (5) analyzing elements and relationships, (6) clarifying and judging alternatives, and (7) summarizing a solution or selecting a course of action. Within this problem-solving process a number of specific thinking skills (e.g., ability to identify the adequacy of data) and affective behaviors (e.g., objectivity) are involved, as well as lower-level cognitive outcomes (e.g., knowledge of concepts) and general problem-solving strategies (e.g., observing, asking questions).

Figure 5.1 presents a collection of specific thinking skills at the levels of analysis, synthesis, and evaluation; these will provide you with flexibility in writing instructional objectives in the area of higher-level thinking. The examples make it possible to select a comprehensive list of specific skill outcomes when focusing on a major problem, or to select a few for a more limited use. Also, the vast array of specific skills in the collection provides for variation from one area to another. For example, analysis in science, social studies, English, mathematics, art, music, and vocational courses are likely to emphasize different specific skills because of the nature of the content or the types of problems to be solved. Similar differences will be found at the levels of synthesis and evaluation. Although the lists of specific thinking skills in Figure 5.1 are not exhaustive, they provide a good starting point for writing objectives in this important area.[1]

Listing the array of specific thinking skills in Figure 5.1 separately does not imply that they should be taught and tested apart from course content. In some cases, a specific thinking skill (e.g., distinguishes between fact and opinion) might be tested and taught separately before it is applied to a particular problem involving analysis. But more commonly, the specific skills will be taught and tested in relation to particular problems or situations in a specific content area. As with other specific learning outcomes, the thinking skills describe how students are to react and the content area describes the types of situations and problems they are to react to.

In confining our lists of specific outcomes in Figure 5.1 to higher-level thinking skills at the analysis, synthesis, and evaluation levels, however, the following types of outcomes important to problem solving are not included.

1. Lower-level cognitive outcomes (knowledge, comprehension, application). These play an important role in the total thinking process but were covered in the last chapter.

2. General thinking strategies such as asking questions, observing, comparing, and organizing data.

3. Affective outcomes such as attitudes, curiosity, independent thought, honesty, objectivity, open-mindedness, perseverance, respect for evidence, and willingness to suspend judgment. Affective outcomes are an integral part of thinking but will be described later in the chapter.

In some cases it may be necessary to incorporate into a description of an objective involving thinking skill outcomes some elements of lower-level outcomes (e.g., interpretation), general thinking strategies (e.g., asks questions), or affective outcomes (e.g., curiosity). There is no attempt here to isolate them except as a basis for discussion and illustration.

---

[1]For a more comprehensive and detailed description of a framework for thinking see Marzano et al., 1988.

Figure 5.1 Examples of Specific Thinking Skills

ANALYSIS

Identifies—

adequacy	contradictions	inconsistencies	reasoning
assumptions	criteria	inferences	relationships
attributes	defects	limitations	relevance
bias	distortions	main ideas	stereotypes
causes	effects	nature of evidence	superstition
central issues	elements	organization	trends
completeness	errors	plausibility	validity
concepts	exceptions	problems	variables
consequences	fallacies	procedures	

Distinguishes between—

accurate and inaccurate	facts and value statements
cause and effect	plausible and implausible
consistent and inconsistent	possible and probable
dominant and subordinate	relevant and irrelevant
essential and inessential	summaries and conclusions
facts and conclusion	supportive and contradictory
facts and hypotheses	valid and invalid
facts and inferences	verifiable and unverifiable
facts and opinions	warranted and unwarranted

Infers—

assumptions	characteristics	motives	purposes
attitudes	conditions	organization	qualities
biases	moods	points of view	relationships

SYNTHESIS

Formulates—

classification systems	generalizations	principles
concepts	hypotheses	problems
conclusions	musical compositions	questions
designs	plans	stories
equations	poetry	summaries
explanations	predictions	theories

EVALUATION

Generates—

criteria	standards	procedures

Judges—

accuracy	correctness	significance
adequacy	credibility	standards
appropriateness	organization	usefulness
clarity	reasonableness	validity
cohesiveness	reasoning	values
completeness	relationships	worth
consistency	reliability	

Making a Useful List of Outcomes

Stating outcomes that are applicable to many types of content make them useful with different units or areas of instruction. The following lists, for example, will indicate how students are to perform when they demonstrate thinking skills in reading, evaluating an argument, or planning an experiment. The statements are general enough to be used with various types of reading and course material.

1. Demonstrates thinking skills in reading.
    1.1 Distinguishes between main ideas and supporting details.
    1.2 Distinguishes between facts and opinions.
    1.3 Distinguishes between facts and inferences.
    1.4 Identifies cause–effect relations.
    1.5 Identifies errors in reasoning.
    1.6 Distinguishes between valid and invalid conclusions.
    1.7 Identifies assumptions underlying conclusions.

2. Evaluates arguments for and against a proposal.
    2.1 Identifies the accuracy of statements.
    2.2 Identifies bias in statements.
    2.3 Distinguishes between relevant and irrelevant statements.
    2.4 Distinguishes between supportive and nonsupportive statements.
    2.5 Identifies the assumptions underlying an argument.
    2.6 Identifies the adequacy of an argument.
    2.7 Identifies the consistency of the facts supporting an argument.
    2.8 Identifies the credibility of sources cited in an argument.

3. Prepares a plan for an experiment.
    3.1 Identifies the problem to be solved.
    3.2 Formulates questions relevant to the problem.
    3.3 Formulates hypotheses in appropriate verbal or mathematical form.
    3.4 Describes controls for variables.
    3.5 Formulates experimental procedures.
    3.6 Formulates observation and measurement procedures.
    3.7 Describes the methods of data analysis.
    3.8 Describes how the results will be presented.

Other specific outcomes could be stated for these general objectives to make them more comprehensive and detailed, or to adapt them to a particular type of reading, experiment, or proposal. These lists, however, indicate the approximate amount of detail needed for clarifying what students can do when they have achieved these higher-level learning outcomes.

Adapting Statements to Areas of Instruction

Although you should try to write the statements of specific thinking skills so that they are applicable to various units of study, the statements still must be in harmony with the area of instruction in which they are used. This can be accomplished by the careful selection and writing of the specific learning outcomes used to describe the general instructional objective. For example, the same general objective might be described in social studies and mathematics as follows:

1. Demonstrates ability to solve problems (social studies).
    1.1 Identifies the main idea in the problem.
    1.2 States the problem in question form.
    1.3 Selects relevant source materials.
    1.4 Analyzes source materials to obtain answers to the problem.
    1.5 Distinguishes between noncausal relations and cause–effect relations.
    1.6 Summarizes the findings from the source material.
    1.7 States conclusions that answer the problem question.
2. Demonstrates ability to solve problems (mathematics).
    2.1 Analyzes a word problem.
    2.2 Identifies the information relevant to solving the problem.
    2.3 Translates words into numerals and symbols.
    2.4 Formulates an equation that represents the problem.
    2.5 Estimates the approximate answer to the problem.
    2.6 Solves the equation to answer the problem.
    2.7 Verifies the problem answer using an alternate method.

The intended learning outcomes may, of course, be more closely adapted to a particular area of instruction by also modifying the general instructional objective. Here we are simply showing how a common instructional objective can be adapted by altering the specific types of student performance that represent the "ability to solve problems."

Adapting Statements to Levels of Instruction

As with lower-level cognitive outcomes, higher-level thinking objectives can be adapted to the various levels of instruction by (1) modifying the lists of specific learning outcomes, (2) varying the difficulty of the problem to be solved or the content to be evaluated, or (3) modifying both the general objective and the specific learning outcomes.

Instruction at the elementary level typically uses fewer and more simply stated specific learning outcomes to define an instructional objective. Thus, if we were to define the instructional objective in reading, illustrated earlier, we might prepare a list such as the following:

1. Demonstrates thinking skills in reading.
    1.1 Identifies the main ideas in a story.
    1.2 Distinguishes between stated details and implied information.
    1.3 Describes the sequence of events in the story.
    1.4 Tells why particular events happened in the story.
    1.5 Describes why the characters acted as they did.
    1.6 Summarizes the meaning of the story.

The earlier objective "Evaluates arguments for and against a proposal" provides an example of how the same objective and list of specific learning outcomes can be used at different levels of instruction by varying the difficulty of the problems or content to be evaluated. Relatively simple proposals can be selected for use at lower levels of instruction and more complex proposals regarding social, economic, or political issues can be used at higher levels. Although the specific learning outcomes may need to be varied slightly to fit different instructional levels or issues, the specific learning outcomes listed earlier for this objective are widely adaptable.

With some modification and simplification of the specific learning outcomes listed for the objective "Prepares a plan for an experiment," it would be possible to use the objective at the elementary level. In some cases, however, it would be desirable to modify the general objective to indicate an experiment for a particular problem and to list the specific outcomes in terms of that problem as follows:

1. Designs an experiment to prove that a plant grows better in some soils than in others.
    1.1 Predicts the type of soil in which plants grow best.
    1.2 Describes each type of soil to be used.
    1.3 Describes the factors to be considered in plant selection.
    1.4 Lists the factors to be kept constant.
    1.5 Describes the measurement procedures to be used.
    1.6 Describes the procedural steps and length of the experiment.
    1.7 Describes how the results will be presented.

Stating the objective and specific learning outcomes as specific as this does not permit their use with other problems, although the general pattern of specific statements does provide a guiding framework. Also, in stating the experimental problem as part of the objective, the students, of course, are not given practice in problem identification. Finally, in simplifying the statements care must be taken not to reduce the student performance from a higher-level thinking skill to a lower-level routine activity.

Affective Components of Thinking

Thinking involves both cognitive and affective components. Until now we have limited our descriptions and illustrations of thinking outcomes to the cognitive area. Here we shall focus on the affective aspects of thinking. Although they are separated for discussion purposes, they are, of course, integrated in various ways in practice.

A collection of some of the more common types of specific affective behaviors associated with thinking skills are shown in Figure 5.2. These lists make it possible to select those that are most appropriate for a particular situation. In some cases they might be included as part of a separate objective concerned with attitudes or dispositions that support thinking skills, as illustrated by "Displays a scientific attitude" in Chapter 6. In other cases, as illustrated in this section, they might be included along with cognitive components in describing the application of thinking skills to some content area or some type of problem solving. As with the cognitive components of thinking, a particular objective may include relatively few affective behaviors or a large number, depending on the nature of the objective, the level of instruction, and the type of problem or situation.

In defining the application of thinking skills to the solution of problems, the cognitive components and affective components can become closely integrated, resulting in a list of specific outcomes as follows.

1. Applies thinking skills in solving social problems
    1.1   Identifies a common social problem.
    1.2   Analyzes the problem and related issues.
    1.3   States the problem and issues clearly.

Figure 5.2   Examples of Specific Affective Behaviors in Thinking

Demonstrates—
    care in observing
    curiosity
    independent thought
    integrity
    objectivity
    open-mindedness

originality
perseverance
respect for evidence
willingness to suspend judgment
willingness to revise opinions

Disposition to seek—
    alternative answers
    confirming data
    contrary points of view
    credible sources

natural causes
reasons for events
relevant information
verifiable facts

Appreciates importance of—
    a clearly stated problem
    care in observation
    commitment to the task
    extending effort
    orderly procedures
    sampling effect on findings

social consequences of findings
persistence
preciseness of results
questioning of results
verification of results
viewpoints of others

1.4   Gathers relevant information from credible sources.

1.5   Distinguishes between facts and opinions.

1.6   Identifies bias and other distortions in statements.

1.7   Seeks viewpoints of others on the problem.

1.8   Suspends judgment until information is complete.

1.9   Identifies factors causing and contributing to the problem.

1.10   Describes possible solutions to the problem.

1.11   Describes the need for social action.

Note that although an attempt was made to define this objective in performance terms, affective elements pervade the statements. We can infer from the statements, for example, that the importance of a clearly stated problem is recognized (1.3), that there is a disposition to seek relevant information and use credible sources (1.4), that objectivity is being sought (1.5 and 1.6), that the viewpoints of others (1.7) and suspending judgment (1.8) are considered important, and that there is a disposition to seek causes (1.9) before obtaining solutions to a problem. Our inferences concerning these affective outcomes will, of course, require more than this one sample of behavior before they can be accepted as evidence of consistent tendencies or dispositions. All we are attempting to do here is to illustrate how affective outcomes might be included when defining thinking skills in problem solving.

Summary

1. Higher-level thinking skills are commonly discussed in the literature under such headings as critical thinking, creative thinking, and problem solving.

2. A learning outcome in a particular area may involve elements from different types of thinking (e.g., both critical and creative).

3. A list of specific thinking skills at the analysis, synthesis, and evaluation levels provides a basis for combining the skills in various ways to fit a particular problem or situation.

4. Be flexible when writing objectives at the thinking level. Avoid describing thinking as a fixed set of skills and strategies.

5. Instructional objectives at the thinking level require that the problems or situations be new to the students.

6. Write instructional objectives that are in general enough terms that they can be used with various units of study.

7. Adapt general thinking objectives to different areas or levels of instruction by modifying the list of specific skill outcomes, or modifying both the general objectives and the specific outcomes.

8. When writing instructional objectives at the thinking level, don't neglect the affective components of thinking. These might be stated as a separate objective (e.g., "Displays a scientific attitude") or might be combined with cognitive elements.

Chapter 6

Writing Objectives for Affective Outcomes

After reading this chapter, you should be able to:

1. Describe the factors that make writing affective objectives so difficult.
2. Distinguish between well-stated and poorly stated affective objectives.
3. Write sample specific learning outcomes in the affective area that reflect observable behavior and those that reflect inner feelings only.
4. Write an affective instructional objective and set of specific learning outcomes for a particular area and level of instruction.
5. Describe why it might be necessary to consider the types of assessment to be made when writing affective objectives.

Preparing intended learning outcomes is more difficult in the affective area than in the cognitive area for a number of reasons. First, the terminology used in this area is vague. Affective outcomes are concerned with feelings and emotions that are described by an individual's disposition, willingness, preferences, enjoyments, and similar terms that have a wide range of meanings and are difficult to describe in performance terms. Second, although some of the intended outcomes can be stated overtly (e.g., "Asks questions") others are covert and can only be inferred (e.g., "Feels confident"). In the latter case, all we can do is state the types of behavior that best support the presence of the inferred characteristic. Third, affective outcomes are described in so many ways. In the literature they are typically classified under such headings as attitudes, interests, appreciations, and adjustments. The affective domain of the *Taxonomy of Educational Objectives* (Krathwohl, Bloom, & Masia, 1964), on the other hand, cuts across these categories and describes behavior within them, ranging from simple responses to complex behavior patterns. An "interest" response, for example, may vary from a person being simply aware that an activity exists to a strong preference for engaging in it. Fourth, as affective behaviors move from simple to complex, as in the *Taxonomy*, they become increasingly internalized and integrated with other behaviors (both affective and cognitive) to form complex value systems and behavior patterns. Thus, at higher levels it is more difficult to isolate and state intended learning outcomes in specific terms without destroying their integrated nature. Also, at higher levels overt responses are less dependable as evidence of internal states. For example, individuals may feel insecure but act completely confident.

Basing Statements on the *Taxonomy* Categories

One way to start is to review the categories in the affective domain of the *Taxonomy* and use these categories as a guide. This procedure might result in statements such as the following:

1. Participates in classroom activities (Receiving and Responding).
    1.1 Listens attentively.
    1.2 Asks relevant questions.
    1.3 Participates in classroom discussion.
    1.4 Volunteers for special tasks.
    1.5 Contributes material for the bulletin board.
    1.6 Helps others when requested.
2. Shows concern for the welfare of others (Valuing).
    2.1 Asks others if they need help.
    2.2 Helps others with their problems.
    2.3 Shares materials with others.
    2.4 Encourages others to do well.
    2.5 Meets obligations in doing group work.
    2.6 Assists those reluctant to participate in group work.
    2.7 Obtains permission before using others' materials.
    2.8 Thanks and commends others, when appropriate.
3. Formulates a rationale concerning the role of society in conserving natural resources (Organization).
    3.1 Relates the needs of society to the conservation of resources.
    3.2 Describes the probable effects on society if resources are wantonly used.
    3.3 Describes the probable effects on society if the use of resources is overly restricted.
    3.4 States personal position reflecting a reasonable balance between the needs of society and the needs to conserve resources.
4. Respects the scientific process (Characterization).
    4.1 Favors evidence that results from scientific studies.
    4.2 Seeks objectivity in the interpretation of evidence.

4.3 Changes opinions when evidence is contrary to beliefs.

4.4 Suspends judgment when evidence is inadequate.

4.5 Shows skepticism when statements are unsupported.

4.6 Questions evidence derived from inadequate studies.

4.7 Bases ideas and opinions on the best scientific evidence available.

These examples illustrate some of the difficulties mentioned earlier in stating affective outcomes. At the lower levels, the specific learning outcomes can be more easily stated in terms of overt behavior that can be observed by the teacher. At the higher levels, where the desired behavior becomes more internalized and integrated, the descriptive terminology becomes more vague and refers to feelings and attitudes. This typically requires assessment by means of self-report methods and other techniques for getting at an individual's internal state.

Basing Statements on Traditional Categories

Because affective outcomes are typically described in the literature under the categories of attitudes, interests, appreciations, and adjustments, some teachers prefer to state objectives using these frameworks. When this is done, the *Taxonomy* can still be useful by helping in the statement of specific learning outcomes. With our two-step method of defining intended learning outcomes, a general instructional objective (e.g., "Shows interest in reading") may be useful at different levels of instruction, but the specific learning outcomes clarify the types of performance expected at a particular level. Thus, the *Taxonomy* can assist in stating the specific outcomes at the appropriate performance level.

Attitudes are probably the most common affective outcome stressed by teachers. Although the major emphasis in teaching may be on cognitive outcomes or skill learning, most teachers want their students to develop a favorable attitude toward their area of instruction and toward learning in general. In addition, other attitude outcomes may constitute an important component of the course. In science courses, for example, the development of a scientific attitude is typically a major objective of the instruction. The following example illustrates how this objective might be defined by a list of specific learning outcomes.

1. Displays a scientific attitude.

    1.1 Demonstrates curiosity in identifying problems.

    1.2 Seeks natural causes of events.

    1.3 Demonstrates open-mindedness when seeking answers.

    1.4 Suspends judgment until all evidence is available.

    1.5 Respects evidence from credible sources.

    1.6 Shows objectivity in analyzing evidence and drawing conclusions.

    1.7 Shows willingness to revise conclusions as new evidence becomes available.

The following statements of intended learning outcomes illustrate how objectives might be written for other traditional categories found in the literature.

2. Demonstrates interest in mathematics.

   2.1 Asks questions that indicate curiosity about math.

   2.2 Asks for extra problems to solve.

   2.3 Completes assignments on time.

   2.4 Brings examples of math problems to class.

   2.5 Helps others with math problems.

   2.6 Seeks ways to improve math learning.

   2.7 Uses math in out of-school-activities.

   2.8 Asks about careers in math.

3. Appreciates good literature.

   3.1 Describes the differences between good and poor literature.

   3.2 Distinguishes between selections of good and poor literature.

   3.3 States reasons for classifying a selection as good or poor.

   3.4 Selects and reads good literature during free-reading period.

   3.5 Explains why he/she likes the selections that are read.

   3.6 Describes his/her emotional reactions to the selections.

   3.7 Expresses a desire for more time to read good literature.

4. Demonstrates good social adjustment.

   4.1 Interacts harmoniously with others.

   4.2 Shares ideas with others.

   4.3 Confines classroom discussions to the issues.

   4.4 Shows concern for the needs and feelings of others.

   4.5 Is selected by others for group activities.

   4.6 Cooperates with others in carrying out activities.

   4.7 Is trustworthy in dealing with others.

   4.8 Is courteous and considerate in working with others.

Of course, many other types of objectives could be listed here. All we are attempting to do is illustrate the various ways that objectives might be stated and defined in the affective area.

In some cases it might be necessary to consider the types of assessment to be made when writing objectives. If observations are to be the main method of evaluating the intended outcomes (e.g., using rating scales or checklists), then it will be necessary to attempt to state the specific outcomes in terms of overt behavior only. If self-report instruments are to be used (e.g., attitude scales and interest inventories), then the statements can include more emphasis on feelings, opinions, preferences, and other internal states. For some types of outcomes both methods of assessment may be appropriate.

Adapting Statements to Areas and Levels of Instruction

As with other types of intended learning outcomes, affective objectives can be adapted to various areas and levels of instruction by selecting specific learning outcomes that best describe the objective in a particular situation. For example a common objective like "Demonstrates a positive attitude toward learning" can be adapted as follows:

1. Demonstrates a positive attitude toward learning (elementary math).

    1.1 Listens attentively when problems are explained.

    1.2 Follows directions when solving problems.

    1.3 Works independently when solving problems.

    1.4 Asks questions when a procedure is not clear.

    1.5 Completes class assignments on time.

2. Demonstrates a positive attitude toward learning (secondary English).

    2.1 Listens attentively during class discussions.

    2.2 Asks questions and makes comments that show interest.

    2.3 Participates eagerly in reading and writing projects.

    2.4 Uses the dictionary whenever needed.

    2.5 Works independently on assigned projects.

    2.6 Completes homework assignments on time.

    2.7 Willingly accepts teacher's criticisms and suggestions on assigned projects.

These sample objectives are, of course, merely intended as illustrations of how to adapt the same objective to a particular situation and do not imply that affective objectives should be stated in a standard way. In many cases, it is more desirable to modify both the general objective and the specific learning outcomes.

Summary

1. Writing objectives in the affective area is more difficult than in the intellectual areas because of the vagueness of terminology, the need to infer covert behavior (e.g., feelings), the numerous ways affective outcomes can be classified, and the fact that the more complex affective outcomes are so closely integrated with other behaviors that they are difficult to isolate and state in specific terms.

2. Affective objectives can be written in terms of the *Taxonomy of Educational Objectives* categories, or the traditional categories of attitudes, interests, appreciations, and adjustments.

3. Write affective objectives in terms of overt behavior whenever possible, but don't neglect inner feelings if important.

4. Use terminology as precise as possible when defining affective objectives, but don't neglect important outcomes just because they cannot be defined in precise terms.

5. When defining some general instructional objectives, it may be necessary to combine both cognitive and affective statements in the same list of specific learning outcomes.

6. Consider the assessment procedures to be used when stating affective objectives (e.g., observation versus self-report).

Chapter 7

Writing Performance Objectives for Skills and Products

After reading this chapter, you should be able to:

1. Describe the importance of considering performance skills when writing instructional objectives.
2. Write an objective and set of specific performance outcomes that focuses on a procedure.
3. Write an objective and set of specific performance outcomes that focus on a product.
4. Write objectives and sets of specific performance outcomes that focus on both procedure and product.

Instructional outcomes concerned with performance skills play an important role in the instructional program. At the primary level, there are numerous tasks that focus on skilled performance, such as speaking, handwriting, reading aloud, drawing, and singing. At the higher levels of instruction, performance outcomes include laboratory skills, communication skills, and various specialized performance skills in agriculture, art, business, home economics, industrial education, music, and physical education. In recent years, instructional outcomes have also focused on problem-solving performance in all areas of study, as a means of integrating learning and applying it to problems like those in the "real world".

In this chapter, we shall be concerned with how to state the more traditional objectives for performance skill and products. Chapter 8 will be concerned with stating performance objectives for problem-solving projects. In both chapters, our sample objectives and lists of specific performance outcomes are best viewed as models or guides.

They illustrate the procedure for stating performance outcomes, but they are stated in broad terms and may need to be modified to fit a particular situation.

Despite their significance as valued learning outcomes, performance skills have been frequently neglected in the past when writing objectives and planning for the assessment of student learning. This is due, at least in part, to the difficulty and time-consuming nature of performance assessment and the subjectivity in judging performance skills. Although performance assessment is a difficult task, it can be made easier by clearly specifying the intended outcomes. The specific performance outcomes can then serve as criteria for scoring or judging student performance. Clearly stated performance outcomes can also contribute to student learning, by communicating to them what is involved in an effective performance, and by providing guidelines for self-assessment of learning progress.

When preparing objectives in this area, it is possible to focus on either:

1. the procedures or process during the performance.
2. the product resulting from the performance.
3. both the procedures and the product.

In giving a speech, for example, the performance itself is important. In writing a theme, however, the product is the focus of attention. The procedures can vary considerably in producing a high-quality theme. However, in some areas, such as typing, emphasis is given to both the procedures (e.g., use of the touch system) and the product (e.g., well-typed letters). We shall describe and illustrate how to write objectives in each of the three areas.

Writing Objectives for Procedure Outcomes

In stating and defining performance objectives, the focus should be on the performance itself (e.g., process) when:

1. The act of performing is the main outcome, or there is no product.
2. A diagnosis of the performance is needed to improve learning.
3. The performance is based on a collection of elements or series of steps that can be identified.

For any particular performance there are a number of elements, or procedures, that are crucial to a successful performance. Thus in writing objectives in this area you should analyze the performance to identify those elements or procedural steps that define a satisfactory performance. These are then listed as specific learning outcomes under the general objective as follows:

1. Presents an oral report to the class.
    1.1 States the topic at the beginning of the report.
    1.2 Speaks clearly and loud enough to be heard.
    1.3 Uses language appropriate for the report.

1.4 Uses correct grammar.

1.5 Speaks at a satisfactory rate.

1.6 Looks at the class members when speaking.

1.7 Uses natural movements and appears relaxed.

1.8 Presents the material in an organized manner.

1.9 Holds the interest of the class.

2. Uses laboratory equipment properly (science).

2.1 Selects appropriate equipment for an experiment.

2.2 Assembles equipment correctly for the experiment.

2.3 Manipulates equipment as needed during the experiment.

2.4 Measures accurately with proper measuring device.

2.5 Follows safety rules in conducting experiment.

2.6 Uses materials without wasting any.

2.7 Completes experiment within time limits.

2.8 Cleans equipment and returns to proper place.

3. Applies varnish correctly.

3.1 Sands and prepares surface properly.

3.2 Wipes dust from surface with appropriate cloth.

3.3 Selects appropriate brush.

3.4 Selects varnish and checks varnish flow.

3.5 Pours needed amount of varnish into clean container.

3.6 Puts brush properly into varnish (one-third of bristle length).

3.7 Wipes excess varnish from brush on inside edge of container.

3.8 Applies varnish to surface with smooth strokes.

3.9 Works from center of surface toward the edges.

3.10 Brushes with the grain of the wood.

3.11 Uses light strokes to smooth the varnish.

3.12 Checks surface for completeness.

3.13 Cleans brush with appropriate cleaner.

3.14 Does *not* pour excess varnish back into can.

3.15 Cleans work area.

In reviewing these objectives, note that in some cases the order of the specific learning outcomes is not especially important (e.g., oral report), whereas in others they define a systematic, step-by-step procedure (e.g., the application of varnish). Where order of procedure is significant in the performance, place the outcomes in the proper order under the objective. This will make it easier to judge the performance and to detect errors.

When specific learning outcomes are properly stated, they can be easily converted to a checklist by simply adding a place to check "yes" or "no" for each procedure, or to a rating scale by adding a place to rate each procedure as it is performed. These instruments can be used both to guide student learning and to evaluate performance. Thus when writing the list of specific learning outcomes, use language that is easily understood by students and that will provide clear statements for checking or rating learning progress.

Writing Objectives for Product Outcomes

Performance objectives should focus on the product resulting from the performance when:

1. The product is the main outcome of the performance.
2. The product has identifiable characteristics that can be used in evaluating the quality of the product.
3. Considerable variation exists in the procedures that can be used in producing the product, or the procedures are not observable to the instructor (e.g., out-of-class work).

If the objective indicates a product and the characteristics of the product can be identified and clearly defined, the specific learning outcomes are stated as criteria that describe a satisfactory product as follows:

1. Constructs a bar graph.
    1.1 Uses a separate bar for each measure.
    1.2 Matches length of each bar to data.
    1.3 Arranges bars in some logical order.
    1.4 Makes bars wider than spaces between them.
    1.5 Uses scale and guidelines that make bars easy to interpret.
    1.6 Identifies each bar with a label.
    1.7 Uses title that clearly indicates the nature of the graph.
2. Writes an effective composition.
    2.1 Expresses ideas clearly.
    2.2 Uses ideas that are logical.
    2.3 Relates ideas to the main thesis.
    2.4 Organizes the thesis to fit the topic.
    2.5 Writes well-structured, relevant paragraphs.
    2.6 Uses parts of speech correctly.
    2.7 Uses words that effectively convey meaning.
    2.8 Spells all words correctly.
    2.9 Uses correct punctuation.

As with procedure outcomes, the list of specific statements defining a product can be easily converted to a checklist or rating scale for use in performance assessment. Keep the statements simple and clear so that the assessment instrument can be used by students, both as a guide to learning and as a basis for self-evaluation.

In addition to being important in general education, products are important in many specialized areas. Courses in art, business, home economics, and industrial education include products that are highly valued as learning outcomes. In most of these areas, however, both the procedures and the product are to be included when defining performance objectives.

Focusing on Both Procedure and Product Outcomes

Performance objectives should include both procedure and product outcomes when:

1. A clear set of procedures exists for producing the product (e.g., cooking recipe, steps in a woodworking project).
2. Learning is at an early stage and the product can be improved by correcting procedural errors.
3. Both the process and the product have identifiable elements that can be described and observed.

Most performance objectives in the school are concerned with entry-level performance. The aim is to learn the proper procedures and to obtain a *satisfactory* level of performance, rather than a high degree of proficiency (unless it's a trade or professional school). Thus, wherever feasible, you should direct your focus toward both the procedures used and the product. By adequately describing the procedures, we can provide guidelines for diagnosing and improving those elements of the performance that will result in a better product. Our description of the product provides a means for evaluating the effect of the improved procedures on the quality of the product and the level of proficiency attained.

A generalized set of specific outcomes for the procedures and product of a woodworking project might be stated as follows:

1. Follows proper procedures.
    1.1 Follows the steps listed in the project plan.
    1.2 Selects appropriate materials to use.
    1.3 Selects proper tools for project.
    1.4 Uses tools correctly for each task.
    1.5 Works carefully to avoid waste of materials.
    1.6 Uses time efficiently and completes project on schedule.
2. Constructs a satisfactory product.
    2.1 Dimensions of product match specifications.
    2.2 Overall appearance reflects care in construction.

2.3 Finish is even and of high quality.

2.4 Joints are smooth and fit tightly.

2.5 Parts (e.g., drawers) fit properly and function well.

These outcomes are stated in general enough terms that they would fit various woodworking projects. When stating outcomes for a particular project, you could, of course, state them in more specific terms.

In some cases, the process and product can be included in the same list of performance outcomes, as follows:

1. Corrects malfunction in electronic equipment.

    1.1 Selects appropriate tools and testing equipment.

    1.2 Applies steps in sequential order.

    1.3 Locates malfunctioning unit.

    1.4 Repairs or replaces malfunctioning unit.

    1.5 Tests equipment for proper functioning.

    1.6 Completes task in reasonable time.

    1.7 Follows safety procedures.

Although the product (i.e., properly functioning equipment) is the main goal, from an instructional standpoint the process is the focus of the performance task. We are assuming, of course, that the testing of the repaired equipment, as important as it is, plays a minor role. If not, we may want to use separate lists of performance outcomes for correcting the malfunction and for testing the repaired equipment. In other cases, we may also want to include a separate list for diagnosing the problem and for following safety procedures. How the intended learning outcomes are organized and stated depends to a large extent on the type and complexity of the performance and on the instructional intent.

In any event, where both procedure and product are important, the performance outcomes should be stated in the manner that is most useful for instruction and performance assessment. This may involve stating them in different ways, to determine which method is best.

Isolating Performance Skills When Writing Objectives

Many types of performance include a combination of cognitive, affective, and skill outcomes (e.g., laboratory work and computer operation). In some cases, it may be desirable to break the performance down into each major type of outcome. For example laboratory performance could be broken down into three separate objectives, as follows:

Knows laboratory procedures (cognitive).

Demonstrates skill in laboratory work (psychomotor).

Demonstrates a scientific attitude when writing and interpreting laboratory results (affective).

With statements such as these, we can describe and assess laboratory work by focusing on each of the three areas. The students' knowledge of procedures can be assessed by testing and observation, the demonstration of skill by a rating of performance, and the scientific attitude by observation, questioning, and examination of the laboratory reports. Such a breakdown enables us to isolate each type of outcome for assessment purposes even though they might be integrated during the instruction.

In other instances, breaking an intended outcome down into separate categories might destroy the integrated nature of the performance. In giving a speech, for example, the content of the speech, the stage presence and gestures used, and the attitudes reflected in the content and delivery of the speech are all part of the effectiveness of the speech and must be assessed as an integrated whole. Although judgments about the content, delivery, and attitudes can be made separately after the speech has been given, they cannot be made apart from any particular speech. In these cases, the intended outcomes should be stated in such a way that they reflect the integrated nature of the activity. They should not be broken down into separate categories just so the statements can be classified as cognitive, psychomotor, or affective.

Guidelines for Writing and Using Performance Objectives for Skills and Products

Although performance outcomes can be stated in many ways, the following guidelines focus on some of the important factors to keep in mind.

1. *Write each general objective so that it focuses on an important procedural skill or product.* The number of objectives will, of course, depend on the nature of the instruction. A simple skill may require only one general objective, whereas a complex performance skill may require several. Each objective should be able to be defined by a limited number of specific performance outcomes.

2. *Write specific performance outcomes that include the most important elements in the performance.* Focus on outcomes that are necessary for successfully demonstrating the performance skill. Don't include peripheral elements that may be present during the conduct of the performance but are not crucial to a successful completion of the task.

3. *Use a sufficient number of specific performance outcomes for each objective to clarify what students can do to demonstrate successful performance.* This means listing enough specific outcomes to define effective performance, but not so many that the observation and judgment of performance becomes burdensome.

4. *State the specific performance outcomes so they can serve as criteria for judging the performance.* This means focusing on observable aspects of the performance rather than on covert, unobservable behavior. For example, use "Follows safety procedures," not "Is safety conscious."

5. *State the specific performance outcomes in terms the students can understand.* If the statements are to provide students with a clear conception of what constitutes successful performance, they must be understood by students.

6. *Share the lists of performance outcomes with students before instruction begins.* This will provide students with a guide for directing their own learning, assessing their own learning progress, and, thus, moving them in the direction of more independent learning—all important aspects of skill development.

Summary

1. Performance objectives are important in most areas of learning but are frequently neglected, due in part to the difficulty and time-consuming nature of performance assessment and the subjectivity in judging performance skills.

2. Performance objectives can focus on the procedure, the product, or both the procedure and the product.

3. When performance objectives are clearly defined, the list of specific performance outcomes can be easily converted to checklists or rating scales for use in the assessment.

4. Performance objectives focusing on procedure should include all specific outcomes that are crucial to a successful performance.

5. When sequence of procedural steps is important, the steps should be listed in proper order.

6. Performance objectives focusing on a product should include characteristics that define a satisfactory product.

7. When performance objectives include both procedure and product, each should be defined by specific performance outcomes.

8. When writing performance objectives, isolate the skill element for descriptive and assessment purposes unless doing so destroys the integrated nature of the activity.

9. Guidelines for writing and using performance objectives for skills and products include writing general objectives that focus on important types of performance and defining each with lists of specific performance outcomes that:

   (a) include the important aspects of the skill or product.

   (b) are sufficient to describe successful performance.

   (c) are stated as criteria for judging the performance.

   (d) are stated in terms students can understand.

   (e) are shared with students before instruction begins.

Chapter 8

Writing Performance Objectives for Problem-Solving Projects

After reading this chapter, you should be able to:

1. Describe the advantages of using problem-solving projects.
2. Distinguish between restricted and extended problem-solving projects.
3. Write performance objectives for a restricted performance project in your instructional area.
4. Write performance objectives for an extended performance project in your instructional area.
5. List guidelines for writing and using performance objectives for problem-solving projects.

Instructional objectives for problem solving are concerned with knowledge, thinking skills, procedures, strategies, and a host of support skills (e.g., research skills, communication skills). This makes the identification and statement of objectives more difficult than in those areas limited to a specific skill or cognitive outcome (e.g., comprehension). The procedure is more manageable if the objectives are stated separately for *restricted* problem-solving projects and *extended* problem-solving projects.

Stating Objectives for Restricted Problem-Solving Projects

Restricted problem-solving projects are limited in scope, highly structured, and typically assigned by the teacher. They can be used in all subject areas, vary from simple to complex, stress the integration and application of learning to realistic-type problems, and provide opportunities for developing higher-level thinking skills. The following examples illustrate the nature of objectives for restricted problem-solving projects.

1. Write a proposal for solving a scientific problem.
    1.1 Describes the nature of the problem.
    1.2 Identifies the scientific concepts and principles involved.
    1.3 Analyzes and interprets relevant source material.
    1.4 Describes a plan for solving the problem.
    1.5 Lists the difficulties involved in carrying out the plan.
    1.6 Predicts the probable effects resulting from the proposed solution.
2. Describes an experiment for comparing two products.
    2.1 Describes the need that the products are designed to meet.
    2.2 Describes a means of testing and comparing the two products.
    2.3 Justifies the procedures used in the testing.
    2.4 Describes the results of the test.
    2.5 Writes recommendations concerning use of the two products.
3. Devises a method for predicting the outcome of an action or event.
    3.1 Describes the action or event.
    3.2 Describes the procedures to be used.
    3.3 Tries out the procedures.
    3.4 Analyzes and interprets the results.
    3.5 Revises the method, as needed.
4. Devises a measurement system using mathematical concepts.
    4.1 Describes the measurement problem.
    4.2 Devises the method of measurement.
    4.3 Explains the system using mathematical concepts.
    4.4 Summarizes the procedure in a mathematical formula.
    4.5 Tests the procedure and describes the results.

These objectives and specific performance outcomes are broadly stated and best serve as templates or models. They can be adapted to a specific area and level of instruction by naming the scientific problem (e.g., reduce smog), the two products (e.g., types of paper towels), the action or event (e.g., basketball game), the measurement problem (e.g., the height of a tall tree) and modifying the specific performance outcomes as needed. Other examples of objectives for problem solving with restricted performance tasks can be found in Chapter 5.

Stating Objectives for Extended Problem-Solving Projects

Extended problem-solving projects are typically designed to enable students to deal with comprehensive, "real world" problems that are poorly structured, have many possible solutions, and require an integration of many types of learning and skill. With an extended problem-solving type of research project, the students are expected to identify and select the problem, design and carry out the study, write a report of the procedure and findings, design an experiment or construct display materials (e.g., model), and present and defend the study before the class or other groups. The performance objectives for the project may be presented to the students or developed cooperatively with them. The criteria for assessing the project are derived directly from the intended performance outcomes and are shared with students before beginning the projects.

Although some schools base the entire curriculum on a problem-solving approach, extended research projects are also usable in a more traditional school curriculum. They are especially useful for developing a variety of performance skills that contribute to independent learning (see Figure 8.1).

The following sample objectives and specific performance outcomes illustrate the types of performance that can serve as a basis for assessing an extended research project, using a written report only.

1. Selects and states a realistic research problem.

    1.1 Lists a number of possible "real world" problems on which to work.

    1.2 Selects a problem that is solvable.

    1.3 Selects a problem that is appropriate for his or her educational background.

    1.4 States the problem clearly and objectively.

Figure 8.1   Problem-Solving Skill Areas

> Following are some of the major skill areas involved in problem-solving projects. They can either be incorporated into the objectives for problem-solving projects, or stated as separate objectives if that seems more desirable. In any event, they should be considered when planning for problem-solving projects.
>
>   thinking skills
>   research skills
>   resource locating skills
>   writing skills
>   display-making skills
>   group-work skills
>   speaking skills
>   self-assessment skills

2. Locates and selects relevant resources.

    2.1 Uses a variety of resources.

    2.2 Selects resource material that is most pertinent.

    2.3 Includes sufficient resource material to draw conclusions.

3. Writes a report describing the project.

    3.1 Describes the problem and nature of the study.

    3.2 Describes the study procedures used.

    3.3 Analyzes, synthesizes, and interprets the findings.

    3.4 Describes possible alternative interpretations of findings.

    3.5 States conclusions that are supported by the findings.

    3.6 Describes the limitations of the study.

    3.7 Lists suggestions for further study.

In some cases a research project is limited to a written report only, as in the previous list. In others, the written report simply provides a background for an experimental study, or it serves as a basis for designing a model, poster, or some other display material. In still other cases, the project is also presented orally to the class and through questioning the student defends the procedures and findings. These more comprehensive projects, of course, require the statement of additional performance outcomes.

The following sample objectives are broadly stated, but illustrate the general nature of the performance outcomes that might be stated for other aspects of a comprehensive research project.

1. Conducts an experimental study.

    1.1 Devises appropriate experimental procedures.

    1.2 Devises controls for variables in the study.

    1.3 Selects and manipulates needed equipment.

    1.4 Uses measurement procedures correctly.

    1.5 Analyzes and interprets the results.

    1.6 Formulates valid conclusions.

2. Prepares display material for the research project.

    2.1 Selects appropriate type of display (e.g., chart, graph, poster, model).

    2.2 Constructs a display that meets criteria for the type of display used.

    2.3 Constructs a display that is relevant to the findings of the research project.

    2.4 Constructs a display that summarizes and clarifies the findings of the research project.

3. Presents and defends the research project before a group.

    3.1 Describes the project in a well-organized manner.

    3.2 Summarizes the findings and their implications.

3.3 Uses display materials to clarify ideas and relationships.

3.4 Answers group members' questions directly and completely.

3.5 Presents a report that reflects careful planning.

3.6 Displays sound reasoning ability through presentation and answers to questions.

Extended research projects may be carried out individually by students or cooperatively in groups. In the latter case, performance outcomes should be stated in terms of how well an individual functioned in the group. For example, you might write statements such as the following:

1. Functions effectively in group work.

    1.1 Participates in the group discussions.

    1.2 Makes comments that are clear, well organized, and relevant.

    1.3 Asks meaningful questions.

    1.4 Listens attentively to the ideas of others.

    1.5 Asks questions and makes comments that reflect thought.

    1.6 Shows respect for other group members.

    1.7 Completes work assigned by group on schedule.

As with the illustrative objectives for the restricted problem-solving projects, these lists of performance outcomes are broadly stated to cover many types of extended problem-solving projects. Thus, they illustrate how to state the performance outcomes, but can best serve as models for stating outcomes that are more specific and relevant to your instructional area.

Guidelines for Writing and Using Performance Objectives in Problem-Solving Projects

If the purpose of problem-solving projects is to integrate various types of learning, developing thinking skills, and encouraging self-assessment and independent learning, the performance objectives should be stated and used in such a way that these intended outcomes are achieved. The following guidelines provide a framework for developing, stating, and using performance objectives in problem-solving projects.

1. *State the performance objectives at the proper level of instruction.* The performance outcomes need to be stated in terms that are understood by the students. Thus at the elementary level of instruction the statements need to be in simpler terminology, briefer and more specific. One way to choose the appropriate terminology is to have students participate in developing the statements. Another is to present your list to students, explain the meaning of the statements, and then modify the statements in terms of the student's comments. Writing, or rewriting, the performance outcomes in terms familiar to students will make them more useful for self-directed learning and self-assessment by students.

2. *Adapt the statements to the area of instruction by using relevant terminology and types of outcomes.* Although performance objectives for problem solving are to encourage the integration of knowledge and skills from many different areas, the statements are more readily understood and viewed as fair, if seen as outcomes relevant to the content area being studied.

3. *Use the specific performance outcomes as criteria for judging performance.* If the outcomes are well stated they can be used directly as criteria or put in question form. For example, a specific outcome concerning a statement of the problem can be restated as follows:

    States the problem clearly and objectively.
    Is the problem stated clearly and objectively?

    Stating the outcomes in question form is usually helpful to students in assessing their own work. In any event, when stating the performance outcomes, you should ask yourself: Is this specific outcome stated well enough to serve as a criterion for guiding learning and assessing the performance?

4. *Develop and make the list of performance outcomes available to students before beginning work on the problem-solving projects.* The list of performance outcomes (i.e., criteria) should be used both in guiding learning and assessing the performance. They should be available to students early so they can be used in directing their own learning, in assessing their own progress, in improving their self-assessment skills, and in achieving independent learning—all goals of the problem-solving projects. A common practice is to have students compare their assessments with those of the teachers and to discuss any discrepancies in judgment. This provides an opportunity to improve both the students' learning and their self-assessment skills. It might also result in modifying some of the criteria to make them more relevant to the projects or more understandable to the students.

5. *Base the instruments to be used to assess learning on the specific performance outcomes.* Procedures for assessing the problem-solving project typically rely on judgments guided by checklists, rating scales, or some type of scoring rubric (i.e., scoring guidelines) describing different levels of performance. The rating or scoring procedure should be based on the criteria derived from the lists of specific performance outcomes.

The procedures for assessing performance outcomes will be discussed and illustrated in Chapter 11. Suffice it here to say that, as a rule, intended performance outcomes and assessment procedures must always be in close harmony, and the assessment procedures should be shared with students at the beginning of the instruction.

Summary

1. Problem-solving projects are useful for integrating learning and skills from many different areas, developing higher-level thinking skills, and providing opportunities for student self-assessment and independent learning.

2. Restricted problem-solving projects are limited in scope, highly structured, and typically assigned by the teacher.

3. Extended problem-solving projects are broad in scope, concerned with poorly structured problems that have many possible solutions (like those in the "real world"), and the students typically are free to select and study a problem of their choice.

4. Extended problem-solving projects may require the statement of performance outcomes for some, or all, of the following areas:

    a. Identifying and selecting a problem.

    b. Locating and selecting relevant resources.

    c. Writing a report describing the project.

    d. Conducting an experiment.

    e. Preparation of display materials.

    f. Oral presentation and defense of the project.

    g. Effectiveness in *group* problem solving.

5. The illustrative objectives and performance outcomes presented in this chapter are broad in scope to fit many types of problems, and are best used as models for stating performance outcomes that are more specific and relevant to a particular instructional area.

6. When writing specific performance outcomes for your instructional area and level of instruction, state them in terms that are clearly understood by students, that reflect the types of problems common to the content area, and that provide clear criteria for judging the performance.

7. Base the procedures used in assessing the problem-solving project directly on the criteria derived from the performance outcomes, and share the intended outcomes and assessment procedures with the students at the beginning of the project. This provides students with a focus for their learning and a basis for assessing their own learning progress.

PART III

Using Instructional Objectives

Chapter 9

Using Objectives in Teaching

After reading this chapter, you should be able to:

1. Distinguish between instructional objectives at the minimum-essentials level and the developmental level.
2. Describe how objectives can be used in instructional planning.
3. Describe a procedure for sharing objectives with students that will provide motivation and direction.
4. Explain how instructional objectives can aid in guiding student learning.

The final list of instructional objectives usually contains some learning outcomes that are considered essential for all students to achieve and others that allow for varying degrees of individual development. In arithmetic, for example, we might expect all students to know multiplication tables, but we anticipate considerable variation in the ability of students to solve problems requiring arithmetical reasoning. Similarly, we may consider it essential for all chemistry students to know the formulas of the chemical compounds studied, but we can expect wide variation in their ability to apply scientific principles to new situations. Learning outcomes that are considered *minimum essentials* are typically low-level outcomes that can be mastered by students. Those outcomes at the *developmental level* represent goals toward which students may show different degrees of progress but which they never fully achieve. The ability to understand, to apply, to interpret, and to think, for example, typically depends on an extended period of development. Their complete attainment is not expected in any given course. All we can expect to do here is to define each objective in terms of those outcomes that are appropriate to the students' learning levels and that represent reasonable degrees of progress toward the objective.

Failure to distinguish between instructional objectives that are considered minimum essentials and those that encourage maximum development has caused considerable confusion in both teaching and assessment. Some teachers tend to treat all objectives as minimum essentials and to strive for mastery on the part of all students. When this is done, the more simple learning outcomes are overemphasized and teaching and assessment tend to focus on specific learning tasks. Other teachers stress objectives at the developmental level only. They put so much emphasis on these more complex learning outcomes that they neglect the knowledge and skills that are useful for attaining higher levels of learning. To avoid these extremes, you should consider both types of objectives when you prepare the list of intended learning outcomes, and you should use teaching and assessment procedures that accommodate both types of outcomes.

Instructional Objectives at the Minimum-Essentials Level

The teaching emphasis at the minimum-essentials level is on shaping and modifying student behavior to fit a predetermined and clearly defined minimum level of performance. The learning outcomes are usually specific and call for simple, independent responses. In fact, the objectives are frequently stated as tasks to be performed rather than as goals to work toward. Thus we might have statements such as the following:

Adds single-digit whole numbers.
Identifies symbols used on weather maps.
Defines basic terms of unit.
Identifies parts of the microscope.

Such simple and clearly defined tasks make it possible to have a one-to-one relation between the stated objective, the teaching procedure, and the testing procedure. As illustrated in the following diagram, the specific learning outcome is stated, the specific task is directly taught, and the specific task is directly tested:

This is the model used in programmed learning and in teaching at the training level. This model is useful for illustrating the direct relationship among objectives, teaching, and testing in the learning of minimum essentials—that is, in areas of learning where the desired outcome is to make all students perform alike at a specified *minimum* level. This model is inappropriate, however, for teaching and testing at the developmental level, as we shall see shortly.

Instructional Objectives at the Developmental Level

The teaching emphasis at the developmental level is on encouraging each student to progress as far as possible toward predetermined goals. The instructional objectives here are typically more general than those at the minimum-essential level. Rather than being stated as specific tasks to be performed, each objective represents a whole class of responses. Thus, the objectives provide direction for both the teacher and the student, without being overly restrictive with regard to the nature of the instruction or the types of learning activities to be engaged in by the student. They allow for openness and exploration in the teaching–learning process that is absent in the closely prescribed shaping and molding process characteristic of the teaching of minimum essentials.

Because each instructional objective at the developmental level represents a large class of specific responses, all we can do in defining each objective is to list a reasonably adequate *sample* of the specific learning outcomes. This process was described in Chapter 3 and is illustrated as follows:

1. Comprehends scientific principles.
    1.1. States the principle in his or her own words.
    1.2. Gives an example of the principle.
    1.3. Identifies predictions that are in harmony with the principles.
    1.4. Distinguishes between correct and incorrect applications of the principle.

The four specific learning outcomes listed under this objective help clarify what is meant by "Comprehends scientific principles," but these are just four of the numerous ways that *comprehension* might be shown. Therefore, these four specific types of response are representative of the variety of responses that could describe the general objective. Because we are able to list only a sample of the types of performance we are interested in, these specific learning outcomes are not expected to be taught and tested one to one. In fact, were this method to be followed, learning would be of a rote nature, and responses could not be used as evidence of *comprehension*. For example, if we were to teach a student to "state a principle in your own words" and later ask the student to "state the principle in your own words," the student's response would represent nothing more than the *recall* of previously learned material. The same would hold true for the other three specific learning outcomes. If all intended outcomes were taught in this manner, we would be functioning at a simple recall level, and the usefulness of the sample of performance as an indication of *comprehension* would be destroyed. That is, the students would be able to demonstrate the types of performance included in the sample (by rote) but would not be able to demonstrate the other types of performance also encompassed by the same instructional objective.

Teaching at the developmental level must be directed toward the general instructional objective and the total class of responses that it represents. The list of specific learning outcomes is mainly useful in providing an operational definition of the general objective and in providing guidelines for assessing learning.

The relation of teaching and assessment to the objectives at the developmental level is illustrated as follows:

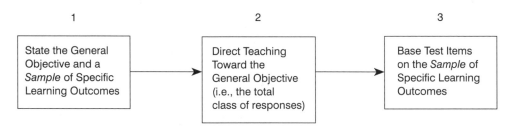

Note that the sample of specific learning outcomes identified in Step 1 can also be used as a basis for developing the test items in Step 3. In measuring such complex learning outcomes as comprehension, however, the test items should go beyond what has been directly taught in Step 2. In stating examples of a principle, for instance, the students should be required to state new examples (i.e., examples not discussed in class). Similarly, the application of principles should be concerned with new situations, and the interpretation of data should be based on data new to the students. It is only when the test items contain some novelty that we are able to go beyond the simple recall level of learning and to measure the more complex learning outcomes.

A summary of some of the major differences between teaching and assessment at the minimum-essentials level and at the developmental level is presented in Table 9.1.

Using Objectives in Instructional Planning

The final list of objectives for a particular course or unit of work specifies the learning outcomes that are to result from the instruction. As we have noted, some of these outcomes will indicate a minimum level of performance required of all students, and some will indicate goals toward which varying degrees of progress can be expected. In any event, these objectives constitute the learning outcomes that are considered to have the greatest value for the students; therefore, they provide a sound basis for instructional planning. To be most effective, of course, the instructional objectives should be identified and defined before other instructional plans are made. When we select both the methods and materials of instruction and the procedures for assessing student progress in light of the intended learning outcomes, we can expect them to be more relevant and more effective.

One way to ensure that the instructional objectives, the teaching methods, and the assessment procedures will be in harmony is to prepare a planning chart that includes all three. The two examples in Table 9.2 illustrate the procedure for preparing a planning chart.

In using a planning chart, you must take care to prevent instruction from becoming subdivided into a series of separate teaching acts. The chart makes clear the relationship between the teaching methods, the assessment procedures, and the desired learning outcomes, but you must not infer that each objective should be worked toward

Table 9.1   Summary Comparison of the Relation of Objectives to Teaching and Assessment at Two Different Levels of Instruction

	Minimum-Essential Level	**Developmental Level**
Types of Learning Tasks	Basic skills and simple knowledge outcomes that are useful for further learning. Minimum skills needed to perform some important task safely and effectively.	Complex types of achievement that depend on an integrated response pattern that typically must be measured as a total functioning unit (comprehension, thinking skills).
Teaching Emphasis	Shape and modify student behavior to fit a predetermined *minimum level of performance*.	Encourage and direct each student toward the *maximum level of development* he or she is capable of achieving.
Nature of the Objectives	Limited, specific, and completely defined tasks to be performed.	General objectives that provide direction and are defined by a *representative sample* of specific types of performance.
Relation of Teaching to the Objectives	Teaching is directed toward the specific task stated in the objective. Each *specific task* is taught on a one-to-one basis.	Teaching is directed toward the *general class of responses* that the objective represents, rather than toward the performance included in the particular sample.
Relation of Testing to the Objectives	Each specific task is assessed directly on a one-to-one basis. The assessment requires students to demonstrate responses identical to those learned in class.	Only a *sample* of specific performance is assessed for each objective. The assessment requires students to demonstrate previously learned responses in situations containing some novelty.

separately. "Knowledge of literary terms," for example, may receive direct attention early in the instruction, but this is a goal to work toward throughout the course. Similarly, when students work on "Interpretation of literature," they would also give attention to specific facts concerning the literary work, to speaking and writing skills, to an appreciation of literature, and so on. In classroom instruction, we typically work on several learning outcomes at the same time. What the chart does is to provide an overall plan to assure that each objective will receive the proper share of attention in the instructional process and that the methods of teaching and assessment will be relevant to the attainment of the desired learning outcomes. The chart, therefore, guides our daily lesson planning. In these daily plans, we can provide for the desired integration of the learning experiences and for their placement in proper sequence.

The same type of instructional planning that is illustrated in Table 9.2 should, of course, be done for all instructional objectives. In planning writing projects, for example, the types of writing outcomes, teaching activities, and assessment procedures should be related. Likewise, in planning for performances and problem solving outcomes, the teaching methods and assessment procedures must be in close agreement with the intended outcomes. For example, if reasoning and other thinking skills are clearly stated as specific learning outcomes of these various projects, the teaching methods and assessment procedures must reflect this emphasis. This type of instructional planning makes

Table 9.2   Instructional Planning Chart

Instructional Objectives	Teaching Methods	Assessment Procedures
Knows literary terms 1. Writes textbook definitions. 2. Identifies examples in a literary selection. 3. Uses the terms correctly in oral and written work.	Encourage students to make a "literary dictionary" and to review the definitions periodically. Point out, and ask students to point out, examples during oral reading. Give oral and written assignments requiring use of the terms.	1. Short-answer test 2. Multiple-choice test 3. Observation and evaluation of written work
Interprets literary works 1. Identifies the major and minor themes. 2. States the author's purpose or message. 3. Identifies the tone and mood. 4. Explains why the characters behave as they do. 5. Points out specific parts of the literature that support the above interpretations. 6. Relates the literary work to other writings.	Read a brief literary work to class. Lead off discussion with questions concerning theme, author's purpose, tone, and character development. Analyze the parts of the literary work and show how they support the general interpretations. Generalize the method of analysis and interpretation by applying it to a second work. Have students select a literary work and write a critical analysis and interpretation.	Observation during class discussions. Objective test on specific points in a literary work and on the process of literary analysis. Essay questions calling for interpretations and supporting evidence. Evaluation of student's written reports (using criteria of effective interpretation).

possible the integration of the teaching-learning-assessment process. All are focused on the same types of expected student performance.

Using Objectives to Motivate and Direct Students

Sharing instructional objectives with students can provide a guide for learning by making explicit to them the relationship between learning activities and the intended outcomes. Knowing what types of performance will be expected as a result of instruction is also motivating in that it clarifies the purpose of the various learning activities and provides direction for study. In short, students are provided with clear achievement targets to work toward.

Students should be made aware of the objectives at the beginning of instruction, to give them an overall picture of the intended learning outcomes. This will help them focus their study early and provide a basis for assessing their own learning progress. It is also helpful to share with students how the learning outcomes will be assessed. When using rating scales, checklists, and other means of assessing performance and problem-solving skills, these should also be shared with students before the activities start. With older students, it is often beneficial to have the students help develop the instruments. This provides an excellent opportunity for students to review and discuss the criteria that are most relevant in judging their learning.

Using Objectives in Guiding Student Learning

In addition to using objectives in planning instruction and motivating students, you can also use them in guiding student learning. When objectives are defined in performance terms, they make signs of learning progress, or lack of progress, more apparent. If we are emphasizing thinking skills, for example, it is helpful to know that our thinking objective is defined by such outcomes as "identifies bias and distortions in statements." Such specific descriptions enable us to provide more meaningful learning experiences and to focus on the types of responses that are expected. Similarly, in teaching speech, writing, and other performance skills, knowing the specific types of performance we are striving for in our instruction enables us to use informal classroom observation more effectively and to take corrective action more promptly.

Clearly stated instructional objectives are especially useful in providing feedback to students. This includes immediate feedback in the classroom, as well as more comprehensive feedback from planned assessment activities. The specific learning outcomes for each objective enable us to direct our comments toward specific weaknesses and to suggest remedial steps that focus on the desired outcomes. It also provides us with a means to help students improve their self-assessment skills by sharing with them the basis for our judgments. If we are to develop independent learners, student self-assessment skills become an important learning outcome in its own right.

A list of carefully defined instructional objectives is, of course, also useful in selecting and preparing assessment instruments for appraising and guiding learning. In fact, this use of objectives is so important that the next two chapters are devoted to it.

Summary

1. Some instructional objectives may be concerned with minimum essentials. These are typically lower-level outcomes (e.g., simple knowledge and skills) that can be fully achieved by students and contribute to the development of complex learning outcomes.

2. Learning outcomes at the minimum-essential level are taught and assessed one to one with little variation between what is taught and what is assessed.

3. Instructional objectives at the developmental level are concerned with complex learning outcomes (e.g., comprehension, application, thinking skills) and focus on students achieving the highest level of performance of which they are capable.

4. Instruction at the developmental level is directed toward the class of responses encompassed by an objective and assessment is based on a representative sample of the possible outcomes. An element of *novelty* is also typically included in the assessment.

5. Instructional objectives can aid in instructional planning by providing a guide for selecting the methods and materials of instruction and for selecting appropriate assessment procedures. An instructional planning chart may be useful as a guide.

6. Sharing the instructional objectives and assessment instruments with students can provide motivation and direction by clarifying the intended outcomes resulting from the learning activities. It can also help students develop self-assessment skills that are needed for independent learning.

7. Objectives defined in performance terms can aid instructors in guiding learning by (a) making signs of learning progress, or lack of progress, more apparent and, thus, providing a basis for taking corrective action more promptly, and (b) providing feedback to students that aids in improving both their performance and their self-assessment skills.

8. Instructional objectives are also useful in selecting and preparing assessment instruments, as we shall see in the next two chapters.

Chapter 10

Using Objectives in Achievement Testing

After reading this chapter, you should be able to:

1. Describe how instructional objectives are used in achievement testing.
2. Explain the advantages of using a table of specifications in preparing tests.
3. Summarize the procedure for preparing a table of specifications.
4. Describe how to prepare test items that are relevant to instructional objectives.
5. Describe the procedure for preparing a test item file.

Instructional objectives play a prominent role in the assessment of student achievement. They describe the types of performance students should be able to demonstrate at the end of instruction. Some types of student performance can be assessed by means of paper-and-pencil tests, others require the use of observation and judgment guided by rating scales, checklists, scoring rubrics, or self-report methods. In this chapter, we will describe the use of objectives in achievement testing. In Chapter 11, we will describe their use in assessing performance skills and affective outcomes.

An achievement test is a device for measuring a sample of student performance. To provide a valid measure, the sample must be relevant and representative of what has been taught during the instruction. A satisfactory sample is most likely to be obtained if a systematic procedure is followed during test preparation. The following steps provide a useful procedure for this purpose.

1. State the general instructional objectives to be tested and define them in measurable terms.
2. Make an outline of the course content.
3. Prepare a table of specifications that describes the nature of the test sample.
4. Construct test items relevant to the table of specifications.

Each of these steps will be described and illustrated for a unit in economics.

Preparing the List of Instructional Objectives

When the instructional objectives have been defined by a list of specific learning outcomes stated in performance terms, they clarify the nature of the performance to be called forth by test items. The following list of instructional objectives illustrates how the objectives might be stated for a brief unit. The list is not exhaustive, but it clarifies the procedure for stating objectives for testing purposes.

OBJECTIVES FOR A UNIT IN ECONOMICS

1. Knows basic terms.

    1.1 Relates terms that have the same meaning.

    1.2 Selects the term that best fits a particular definition.

    1.3 Identifies terms used in reference to particular economic problems.

    1.4 Uses terms correctly in describing economic problems.

2. Comprehends economic concepts and principles.

    2.1 Identifies examples of economic concepts and principles.

    2.2 Describes economic concepts and principles in his or her own words.

    2.3 Identifies the interrelationship of economic principles.

    2.4 Explains changes in economic conditions in terms of the economic concepts and principles involved.

3. Applies economic principles to new situations.

    3.1 Identifies the economic principles needed to solve a practical problem.

    3.2 Predicts the probable outcome of an action involving economic principles.

    3.3 Describes how to solve a practical economic problem in terms of the economic principles involved.

    3.4 Distinguishes between probable and improbable economic forecasts.

4. Interprets economic data.

    4.1 Differentiates between relevant and irrelevant information.

    4.2 Differentiates between facts and inferences.

    4.3 Identifies cause–effect relations in data.

    4.4 Describes the trends in data.

    4.5 Distinguishes between warranted and unwarranted conclusions drawn from data.

    4.6 States proper qualifications when describing data.

Note that the statements of specific learning outcomes listed under each general objective describe how the students are expected to react toward the subject matter in economics but do not describe the specific subject matter toward which they are to react. Therefore, the specific statements listed under "Knows basic terms" describe what is meant by "knowing"—not what terms the students should know. Such statements make it possible to relate the objectives and the specific learning outcomes to various areas of content and thus to various units within the same course. As we shall see shortly, the table of specifications provides a method for relating the instructional objectives to the course content.

Outlining the Content

Because an achievement test should also adequately sample the content included in the instruction, an outline of the content is needed for the test. The same content outline that is used for teaching may suffice, or a less elaborate outline may be developed as part of the test plan. The following list of topics for our illustrative unit in economics provides sufficient detail for testing purposes.

CONTENT OUTLINE FOR A UNIT IN ECONOMICS (MONEY AND BANKING)

A. Forms and functions of money
    1. Types of money
    2. Various uses of money
B. Operation of banks
    1. Services provided by commercial banks
    2. Other institutions offering banking services
    3. Role of banks in managing the flow of money
C. Role of the Federal Reserve System
    1. Need for flexibility in the money supply
    2. Nature of the Federal Reserve System
    3. Regulatory policies influencing the money supply
D. State regulation of banks
    1. The state banking commission
    2. Laws to protect the borrowers

The amount of detail to be included in the outline of content will depend on the length of time covered by the instruction. For a two-week unit of work, you may be able to include all of the major and minor topics. In outlining the content for an entire course, however, you may have to limit the outline to the main subject headings. Restricting the length of the outline to one or two pages is usually satisfactory for test-construction purposes.

Preparing the Table of Specifications

A table of specifications is a two-dimensional table that relates the instructional objectives to the course content. The table makes it possible to classify each test item in terms of both objectives and content. A completed table describes the number of test items needed to obtain a balanced measure of the instructional objectives and the course content emphasized in the instruction.

A sample table of specifications, based on our illustrative unit in economics, is shown in Table 10.1. To simplify the table, we have included only the general instructional objectives and major areas of content. This procedure is typical, although more detail may be desirable in some situations.

The numbers listed within the table indicate the number of test items to be constructed in each area. For example, a total of 15 items will measure the objective "Knows basic terms," including 3 items in the content area "Forms and functions of money," 4 in the content area "Operation of banks," and so on down the column. The total number of items in each column indicates the relative emphasis to be given to each objective, and the total number of items in each row indicates the relative emphasis to be given to each area of content. Therefore, the two-way grid specifies the test sample in terms of both instructional objectives and course content.

The relative emphasis shown in the table of specifications should reflect the emphasis given during instruction. This is accomplished by assigning weights to each objective and to each content area during the construction of the table. The usual procedure is first to distribute the total number (or percentage) of test items over the objectives and content areas and then to distribute the items among the individual points. Although a number of factors might be considered in assigning such weights, the amount of instructional time devoted to each area will usually provide a satisfactory approximation. In Table 10.1 for instance, it is assumed that the *Interprets data* (5 test items) received only one-third of the instructional emphasis given to each of the other objectives (15 test items each) and that this instruction was limited to content areas B and C. The table also indicates, by the number of items in each row, that content areas A and D received less instructional emphasis than areas B and C.

Constructing Relevant Test Items

The table of specifications describes the nature of the desired test sample and specifies what each test item should measure. The next task is to construct test items that are relevant to the instructional objectives and content areas of each cell. For example, in using Table 10.1, let's assume that we are going to construct one of the four test items to measure the first objective ("Knows basic terms") in content area B ("Operation of banks"). Our procedure would be as follows: (1) to select one of the specific learning outcomes listed under the first objective, (2) to select one of the important banking terms, and (3) to construct a test item that calls forth the specific performance indicated in the learning outcome. Our test item should clearly reflect the desired learning outcome as follows:

Instructional Objective: 1. Knows basic terms.

Learning Outcome: 1.1. Relates terms that have the same meaning.

1.   Checking accounts are also called

   *A.   demand deposits.

   B.   time deposits.

Table 10.1   Table of Specifications for a 50-Item test in Economics (Money and Banking)

Content Areas	Instructional Objectives			
	1 **Knows** **Basic Terms**	**2** **Comprehends** **Concepts** **and Principles**	**3** **Applies** **Principles**	**4** **Interprets** **Data**
A. Forms and functions of money	3	4	3	
B. Operation of banks	4	3	5	3
C. Role of the Federal Reserve System	4	6	3	2
D. State regulation of banks	4	2	4	
Total number of test items	15	15	15	5

    C. currency.

    D. credit money.

Note in the above example that the learning outcome describes the specific response we expect the students to demonstrate and that the test item presents a relevant task. Other examples at the comprehension and application levels are presented below. The objectives and outcomes are from our illustrative list of objectives for a unit in economics and are numbered accordingly.

Instructional Objective: 2. Comprehends economic concepts and principles.

Learning Outcome: 2.1. Identifies examples of economic concepts.

1.   Which one of the following is an example of commercial credit?

   *A. A manufacturer borrows money to buy raw materials.

    B. A manufacturer borrows money to build a new plant.

    C. A business executive borrows money to build a new house.

    D. A stockbroker borrows money to buy stocks and bonds.

Instructional Objective: 3. Applies economic principles to new situations.

Learning Outcome: 3.2. Predicts the possible outcome of an action involving economic principles.

1.   Which one of the following actions of the Federal Reserve Board would most likely contribute to greater inflation?

   *A. Buying government bonds on the open market.

    B. Raising the reserve requirements.

    C. Raising the discount rate.

    D. Lowering the amount of credit granted to member banks.

Preparing a File of Test Items

You can easily prepare a test item file (called an item bank or item pool) by recording each item on a separate card and placing above it the content area, objective, and specific learning outcome being measured. You can then file the cards by content area, using the objective categories as subheadings. For example, our illustrative unit on banking could serve as a major category, with the subcategories as follows:

Banking:

    Knowledge

    Comprehension

    Application

    Interpretation

This type of filing system is especially important as we construct test items that go beyond the measurement of knowledge outcomes. Items that measure understanding, application, and various thinking skills are time-consuming to construct. Building a file of such items eases the burden of test construction in the future.

If microcomputers are available, the pool of objectives and relevant test items can be stored directly in the computer. In this case, the items are coded by the content, objective, and specific learning outcome measured, as well as the grade level and other relevant characteristics (e.g., item difficulty). When such item pools are stored, the computer can be programmed to select items and build a test with known characteristics. The computer can print out these custom-designed tests and also provide scoring, reporting, and analyzing functions. This relieves the teacher of many of the time-consuming functions of classroom testing.

Item banking by computer is typically a cooperative affair among teachers in a particular department. If computers are not yet available in the school, a card file can be maintained, either individually or cooperatively, and this will provide a pool of items for item banking when computers do become available.

Using Detailed Specifications for Item Writing

When test items are being prepared cooperatively by teachers, as for a departmental examination or for storage in item banks, detailed specifications may be useful for item writing. In this case, the general instructional objective and the specific learning outcomes to be tested are stated, the type of test item to be used is indicated, and characteristics of the item are briefly described and illustrated with a sample test item. Examples of such specifications in two skill areas are presented in the boxes.

The use of detailed specifications provide greater assurances that a functionally equivalent set of relevant test items will be prepared for each specific learning outcome, despite the fact that several teachers are constructing the items. The detail is also useful in clarifying the meaning of the results during test interpretation.

Box 10.1   Writing

General instructional objective: Knows fundamentals of written expression.

Specific learning outcome: Distinguishes between complete and incomplete sentences.

Type of test items: Multiple-choice (10 items)

Item characteristics: Each test item will contain one complete sentence and three incomplete sentences. The *stem* of the item will tell the student to choose the complete sentence. The *correct response* will be a complete sentence. The *incorrect alternatives* (distracters) will be sentence fragments.

Sample item:
Choose the *complete* sentence.
  A. The children who went to the zoo.
  B. The monkeys in the zoo swinging.
*C. Going to the zoo was fun.
  D. Whatever you think of the zoo

Box 10.2   Math

General instructional objective: Comprehends our number system.

Specific learning outcome: Identifies place value

Type of test items: Multiple-choice (10 items)

Item characteristics: Each test item will contain a stem in the form of a question or incomplete statement, followed by four alternative answers. The *stem* of the item will contain a whole number with three to six digits. The student will be asked to identify the value of two of the digits by indicating the degree to which one is a multiple of the other. The *correct response* will indicate an understanding of the place value of both digits. The *incorrect alternatives* (distracters) will consist of common errors in identifying place value.

Sample item:
In the number 9,632, the 9 has a value that is
  A. three times the value of the 3
  B. thirty times the value of the 3
*C. three hundred times the value of the 3
  D. three thousand times the value of the 3

When detailed specifications are used, the table of specifications, discussed earlier, still plays an important role. It provides an overall framework for preparing an item bank and it provides a guide for selecting items from the bank when preparing a test for a particular use.

Summary

1. Instructional objectives play a key role in the testing of student achievement by describing the types of performance to be measured.

2. A table of specifications is a useful guide for constructing a test that measures a relevant and representative sample of student performance.

3. A table of specifications is a two-dimensional table that indicates the nature and number of test items needed to obtain a balanced measure of the intended learning outcomes.

4. Relevant test items are obtained by constructing items that call forth the student performance described in the specific learning outcomes.

5. Preparing a test item file provides a pool of items for future use. If computers are available, the items can be stored directly in the computer for easy retrieval and use.

6. Detailed specifications for writing test items may be useful where teachers are preparing items cooperatively for departmental examinations or storage in item banks.

Chapter 11

Using Objectives in Performance and Affective Assessment

After reading this chapter, you should be able to

1. Describe how instructional objectives are used in performance and affective assessment.
2. Distinguish between analytic and holistic scoring.
3. List the steps in using instructional objectives to construct rating scales, checklists, and scoring rubrics.
4. List the steps in preparing an attitude scale.
5. Describe how instructional objectives can contribute to the use of student portfolios.
6. List the guidelines for preparing and using assessment instruments.

A number of important learning outcomes cannot be measured by the traditional paper-and-pencil test. Most of these require the assessment of performance skills (e.g., communication skills, laboratory skills, vocational skills) or affective outcomes (e.g., attitudes, interests, values). In assessing these types of learning, we need to depend on judgments of the ongoing process, the product resulting from the process, or both. Typically some type of observational instrument (e.g., rating scale or checklist) or scoring guide (e.g., scoring rubric) is used to direct and record our judgments. The method depends to a large extent on the type of information we are seeking and, thus, the scoring procedure to be used.

Assessing Performance Skills

As with testing procedures, the specific learning outcomes for each objective provide the criteria for judging the quality of the performance. In some cases we may want to make separate judgments on each criterion. This provides for *analytical scoring* and uses a recording device such as a rating scale or checklist. The main advantage of this procedure is that it provides a diagnostic picture of a student's strengths and weaknesses, and, thus, provides a basis for improving performance. However, in some cases we may want to consider the criteria as a whole and make an overall assessment of performance. This requires the use of *holistic scoring*.

Holistic scoring classifies the overall performance into one of a number of categories (e.g., Excellent, Good, Acceptable, Inadequate). Each category may be then briefly described by degrees to which the overall criteria have been satisfied. These scoring guides are called *scoring rubrics*. Holistic scoring is defended on the basis that the whole is more than the sum of its parts. In assessing a speech, for example, your impression may be that it was a good speech even though the speaker violated some of the common rules of speaking. Likewise, in assessing a product like writing, you may conclude that it is excellent writing even though the organization, vocabulary, and style do not follow the usual pattern. Thus, this overall impression of the performance or product provides something different from what you would get by simply summing the scores obtained from analytical scoring.

There is, of course, no reason why both holistic and analytic scoring cannot be used for the same performance or product. One provides the overall judgment and the other provides useful diagnostic information. However, where both are used, the overall judgment should be made first so that it is less likely to be distorted by a low rating on some specific element.

Rating Scales

The rating scale provides a convenient observational guide for analytical scoring. It (1) focuses attention on the specific elements of the performance to be observed, and (2) provides a convenient method of recording the judgments of the observer. Typically the rating scale can be easily prepared by using the specific learning outcomes as criteria for judging the performance and adding a scale for rating on each specific item.

Let's assume that the following performance objective and list of specific outcomes have been written for a science course (taken from Chapter 7).

1. Uses laboratory equipment properly.
    1.1 Selects appropriate equipment for an experiment.
    1.2 Assembles equipment correctly for the experiment.
    1.3 Manipulates equipment as needed during the experiment.
    1.4 Measures accurately with proper measuring device.
    1.5 Follows safety rules in conducting experiment.
    1.6 Uses materials without wasting any.

    1.7 Completes experiment on time.

    1.8 Cleans equipment and returns to proper place.

Each of these specific outcomes can serve as items in a *rating scale* by simply modifying the wording slightly and by adding a place beneath each item to record the ratings, as shown in Figure 11.1.

The complete rating scale would include (1) items covering all specific outcomes to be judged, (2) directions for making the ratings, and (3) possibly a place for comments beneath each rating scale item. All we are doing here is illustrating how easy it is to construct a rating scale when the intended outcomes have been clearly specified. The specific outcomes indicate the performance to be observed and become the items in the rating instrument. The graphic scale beneath each item simply provides a place to record the ratings. A more compact type of rating scale can be made by listing a set of numbers in front of each specific outcome and describing the meaning of the numbers in the directions. A scale of this type for the procedures and product of a wood-working project (taken from Chapter 7) is shown in Figure 11.2.

This numerical rating scale, like the graphic scale, again simply uses the stated specific outcomes as the items in the scale. If the outcomes are carefully stated, making a rating scale is a simple task. Also, stating them in terms students can understand makes it possible for students to rate their own performance or product and compare it with the teacher's rating. A conference discussing the discrepancies in ratings can contribute to both improved student performance and improved student self-assessment skills.

Checklists

In assessing some types of performance, the judgment on each performance criterion requires a simple yes-or-no response. For example, in observing a procedure we may be

Figure 11.1 Sample Rating Scale Items

1.1 Selects appropriate equipment

1	2	3	4	5
Needs to be told what equipment to use		Needs some help in selection		Selects proper equipment without aid

1.2 Assembles equipment correctly

1	2	3	4	5
Needs help on most parts of the assembly		Needs help on some parts of the assembly		Completes assembly quickly and correctly

Figure 11.2 Sample Numerical Rating Scale

Directions: Rate each of the following items by circling the appropriate number:
4 = Outstanding, 3 = Good, 2 = Acceptable, 1 = Inadequate

Follows proper procedures

4 3 2 1 (a) Follows the steps listed in the project plan.

4 3 2 1 (b) Selects appropriate materials to use.

4 3 2 1 (c) Selects proper tools for project.

4 3 2 1 (d) Uses tools correctly for each task.

4 3 2 1 (e) Works carefully to avoid waste of material.

4 3 2 1 (f) Uses time efficiently and completes project on schedule.

Constructs a satisfactory product

4 3 2 1 (a) Dimensions of product match specifications.

4 3 2 1 (b) Overall appearance reflects care in construction.

4 3 2 1 (c) Finish is even and of high quality.

4 3 2 1 (d) Joints are smooth and fit tightly.

4 3 2 1 (e) Parts (e.g., drawers) fit properly and function well.

only interested in determining whether a specific action was taken. In judging a product, we may be only concerned about the presence or absence of each specific characteristic. In these cases, the list of performance steps or product characteristics can be assessed by means of a *checklist*.

The checklist, like the rating scale, (1) is derived directly from the list of specific outcomes that describes the procedure or product, (2) directs attention to the significant elements to be observed, and (3) provides a convenient method of recording the observations. The main difference between them is in the type of judgment to be made. The rating scale calls for a judgment concerning the degree to which a characteristic is present, whereas the checklist calls for a present or absent judgment. An illustrative checklist, based on a performance objective in Chapter 7, is shown in Figure 11.3.

Checklists are also useful with those products that require a simple judgment concerning whether a characteristic is present or absent. The list of outcomes for constructing a bar graph (from Chapter 7), for example, does not imply that the degree of each characteristic is important. Therefore, a checklist will suffice, as illustrated in Figure 11.4. Of course, in cases where the degree to which each characteristic is present provides a more adequate assessment of a product, the rating scale should be used.

As with the rating scale, the items listed in a checklist should be stated in terms that are readily understood by students, so they can use the list to check their own performance and develop self-assessment skills.

Figure 11.3 Checklist for Evaluating the Proper Application of Varnish

Directions: On the space in front of each item, place a plus (+) sign if performance is satisfactory, place a minus (–) sign if it is unsatisfactory.

_____ 1. Sands and prepares surface properly.

_____ 2. Wipes dust from surface with appropriate cloth.

_____ 3. Selects appropriate brush.

_____ 4. Selects varnish and checks varnish flow.

_____ 5. Pours needed amount of varnish into clean container.

_____ 6. Puts brush properly into varnish ($\frac{1}{3}$ of bristle length).

_____ 7. Wipes excess varnish from brush on inside edge of container.

_____ 8. Applies varnish to surface with smooth strokes.

_____ 9. Works from center of surface toward the edges.

_____ 10. Brushes with the grain of the wood.

_____ 11. Uses light strokes to smooth the varnish.

_____ 12. Checks surface for completeness.

_____ 13. Cleans brush with appropriate cleaner.

_____ 14. Does *not* pour excess varnish back into can.

_____ 15. Cleans work area.

Scoring Rubrics

As noted earlier, holistic scoring is based on a person's impression of the performance skill or product. When these types of judgments are made, the judges typically place the performance or product into one of several categories. A commonly used number of categories is 4 or 6. An even number is used so that a middle category doesn't become a dumping ground. The judgment and placement in a category is usually aided by a scoring guide called a *scoring rubric*. These scoring rubrics describe the qualities at each level of performance and are derived from the intended performance outcomes. Using scoring rubrics makes it possible to express the level of proficiency by either a descriptive label or a number (e.g., Excellent—4, Good—3, Acceptable—2, and Inadequate—1).

A sample scoring rubric for assessing a written report of a problem-solving project is presented in Figure 11.5. The descriptions for each level are from the list of performance outcomes in Chapter 8. They are more fully stated here than they might be for a scoring rubric, to illustrate their derivation from the stated performance outcomes. In some cases, it may be desirable to modify or abbreviate them for scoring purposes. Just make sure that the key elements are included in the list of criteria.

In some cases, it may be desirable to combine holistic scoring with analytical scoring. For example, a rating scale may be developed for analytical scoring with a place

Figure 11.4   Checklist for Evaluating the Construction of a Bar Graph

Directions: On the space in front of each item, place a plus (+) sign if the characteristic is present, place a minus (-) sign if characteristic is absent.

_____   1.   Uses a separate bar for each measure.

_____   2.   Matches length of each bar to data.

_____   3.   Arranges bars in some logical order.

_____   4.   Makes bars wider than space between them.

_____   5.   Uses scale and guidelines that make bars easy to interpret.

_____   6.   Identifies each bar with a label.

_____   7.   Uses title that clearly indicates nature of the graph.

provided at the beginning for the overall judgment of the performance or product. This makes it possible to record the general impression first and then to clarify the overall judgment by noting strengths and weaknesses on the rating scale items.

Assessing Affective Outcomes

The assessment of affective outcomes is much more difficult than the assessment of cognitive outcomes or performance skills. Students' feelings and emotions are more controlled and may be concealed by expected social behavior. Thus in addition to routine classroom observation, we need to use a variety of assessment techniques to supplement our observations and judgments. Here again, checklists and rating scales are useful, as are self-report methods that attempt to assess students' internal states (e.g., attitudes and interests).

As with performance assessment, the instruments used here should be fashioned from the lists of intended learning outcomes. For example, the items in the checklist illustrated in Figure 11.6 are derived from the list of affective outcomes presented in Chapter 6. These same items could also be used in a rating scale, of course, if *degree* of class participation is the focus. Frequently a simple checklist, like the one in Figure 11.6, is used at the lower elementary level and a more detailed rating scale is used at higher levels of instruction. In either case, however, the items are derived directly from the list of affective outcomes.

Some affective outcomes require the use of self-report methods such as the *attitude scale*. For example, attitude toward school, toward a particular course, toward laboratory work, or some activity may be considered an important learning outcome. Although some information can be obtained by observation, obtaining self-report data concerning attitudes can provide a meaningful supplement to observation.

As with other assessment techniques, the attitude scale should be prepared in harmony with the outcomes to be evaluated. For example, describing in specific terms

Figure 11.5   Scoring Rubric for the Written Report of a Problem-Solving Project

---

4. Description of problem and study procedures is outstanding.

    Thorough analysis, synthesis, and interpretation of findings.

    Clearly stated conclusions that are supported by the findings.

    Comprehensive description of limitations of the study and the need for further research.

3. Description of problem and study procedures is good.

    Fairly thorough analysis, synthesis, and interpretation of findings.

    Conclusions are clear and generally supported by findings.

    Descriptions of limitations of study and the need for further research could be more detailed.

2. Description of problem and study procedures is weak.

    Limited analysis, synthesis, and interpretation of findings.

    Conclusions are rather general and not fully supported by findings.

    Descriptions of limitations of study and the need for further research are brief and general.

1. Description of problem and study procedures is unclear.

    Attempts at analysis, synthesis, and interpretation are incomplete.

    Conclusions are general and not in harmony with findings.

    Description of limitations of study and the need for further research are missing or inadequate.

---

what is meant by a "favorable attitude toward science" provides the basis for selecting statements that are clearly favorable and clearly unfavorable for use in an attitude scale like the one shown in Figure 11.7. This Likert-type scale uses five alternatives and favorable items like the first one are scored by using values of 5, 4, 3, 2, 1, going from SA to SD. In scoring unfavorable items like the second one, the values are reversed to 1, 2, 3, 4, 5, going from SA to SD. An individual's score on this type of scale is the sum of the scores on all items, with a higher score indicating a more favorable attitude. If an intended learning outcome in the area of attitudes has been carefully defined, a Likert-type scale can be easily prepared, scored, and interpreted.

In using self-report methods, such as an attitude scale, it is important that the student responses be obtained anonymously. Students are unlikely to give honest responses if they can be identified. This poses no great problem in assessing students' attitudes, however. We should be mainly interested in how the instruction is changing attitudes, and not which students are changing most. For example, if students' attitude scores become more favorable toward science during the instruction, then we are meeting our objective.

Figure 11.6   Checklist for
Evaluating Class Participation

Directions: Circle YES or NO to indicate your response.			
YES	NO	1.	Listens attentively.
YES	NO	2.	Asks relevant questions.
YES	NO	3.	Participates in classroom discussions.
YES	NO	4.	Volunteers for special tasks.
YES	NO	5.	Contributes material for the bulletin board.
YES	NO	6.	Helps others when requested.

Using Student Portfolios

In some schools, students keep portfolios containing samples of their best work. This might include samples of writing, drawing, math problems, research reports, ratings and checklists of performance skills, and other evidence of school performance. The samples are typically collected and sequenced so that learning progress can be judged (e.g., improvement in writing skills, drawing skills, or problem-solving ability). The portfolio is an especially useful method for communicating to both students and parents the degree of student improvement. Nothing makes clearer the actual changes in student performance than a comparison of sample work obtained at different times during the instruction.

In some instances, a portfolio may be limited to one type of skill (e.g., writing). In others, a portfolio of all classroom work might be assembled for a more complete assessment of learning progress. Regardless of the nature and scope of the portfolio, there are three basic questions to consider in using this technique: (1) What type of student work should be included in the portfolio? (2) Should the samples of student work be based on assigned exercises or should routine classwork be collected? (3) How is the portfolio of student work samples to be assessed? A set of instructional objectives defined in terms of intended learning outcomes can serve as a guide for all three decisions.

The list of instructional objectives makes clear what performance tasks are needed to fill in gaps and supplement paper and pencil testing. For example, a test of knowledge outcomes (e.g., elements of grammar) will need to be supplemented by an assessment of application outcomes (e.g., writing samples). In addition, the specific learning outcomes that define each objective can help decide whether a performance exercise needs to be assigned (e.g., write a short story) or typical samples of classwork should be collected (e.g., daily written work). Finally, the list of objectives and specific learning outcomes can aid in assessing the portfolio samples by specifying the precise nature of the student performance to be judged.

Guidelines for Preparing and Using Assessment Instruments

Throughout this chapter our main goal has been to describe and illustrate how well-defined instructional objectives can be used in assessing performance skills

Figure 11.7   Illustrative Likert-Type Attitude Scale for Measuring Attitude Toward a Science Course

---

Directions: Indicate how much you agree or disagree with each statement by circling the appropriate letter(s).

	SA — Strongly Agree
	A — Agree
KEY	U — Undecided
	D — Disagree
	SD — Strongly Disagree

SA	A	U	D	SD	1.	Science classes are interesting.
SA	A	U	D	SD	2.	Science laboratory is dull and boring.
SA	A	U	D	SD	3.	It is fun working on science problems.
SA	A	U	D	SD	4.	Class activities are good.
SA	A	U	D	SD	5.	Reading the textbook is a waste of time.
SA	A	U	D	SD	6	The laboratory experiments are interesting.
SA	A	U	D	SD	7.	Most class activities are monotonous.
SA	A	U	D	SD	8.	I enjoy reading the textbook.
SA	A	U	D	SD	9.	The problems we are studying are unimportant.
SA	A	U	D	SD	10.	I am *not* very enthusiastic about science.

---

and affective outcomes. When instructional objectives are defined in terms of intended learning outcomes, they clarify precisely what is to be assessed, they provide a guide for selecting and preparing assessment instruments, and they aid in the interpretation of results. If a portfolio is used, objectives can also aid in determining the type of student work to be included and the criteria to be used in assessing the work samples.

The following suggestions provide guidelines to keep in mind when preparing assessment instruments from instructional objectives and using them to improve learning.

1. Check to be sure that the specific learning outcomes include the most important elements of each objective.

2. Use the intended learning outcomes as criteria for preparing the assessment instrument.

3. Select the type of assessment instrument that best evaluates the performance skills or affective outcomes.

4. Prepare an instrument that is understandable and easy to use by students.

5. Use an appropriate scoring procedure (i.e., holistic for overall judgment, analytic for judgment on each criterion).

6. Share the assessment instruments with students before instruction begins and have students use them to assess their own learning progress during instruction.

7. If students are mature enough, have them participate in preparing the assessment instruments.

8. If a portfolio of schoolwork is to be kept by each student, use the instructional objectives and specific learning outcomes as a framework for selecting and assessing the work samples to be included.

Throughout this chapter, and in Chapter 10, the focus has been on how to use objectives and specific learning outcomes in the assessment of learning. No attempt was made to discuss student assessment in any great detail. For more elaborate descriptions and illustrations of how to assess learning outcomes, and for reference to many other books about student assessment, see Linn and Gronlund (2000) and Gronlund (1998). It is simply our contention here that basing assessment on clearly stated intended learning outcomes results in more comprehensive and valid evidence of student learning.

Summary

1. Instructional objectives play a key role in assessing performance skills and affective outcomes by describing the relevant aspects to be judged (i.e., they provide the criteria for assessment).

2. Performance skills may be assessed using analytical scoring (i.e., a separate judgment on each criterion) or holistic scoring (i.e., a general impression of the performance or product).

3. Analytical scoring is typically done by using a rating scale for recording the degree to which an element is present, or by using a checklist that simply requires a present or absent judgment.

4. A rating scale or checklist can be prepared by listing the specific learning outcomes as items to be judged and adding a scale for responding to each item.

5. Holistic scoring typically uses a scoring guide, called a scoring rubric, that classifies the performance or product into one of several categories (e.g., excellent, good, acceptable, inadequate). An even number is used to avoid a middle dumping ground, and 4 or 6 categories are commonly used.

6. Affective outcomes that are observable can be judged with the aid of a rating scale or a checklist. As with performance skills, the items in the observation instrument are derived from the list of specific learning outcomes.

7. Affective outcomes based on inner feelings, such as attitudes, typically are assessed with self-report methods. The attitude scale is probably the most commonly used one in teaching. Its use requires anonymous responses, if the results are to be valid.

8. A portfolio of samples of student work is useful for assessing learning progress and for communicating the amount of improvement to students and parents. Stating

the objectives in performance terms provides a framework for determining what work samples to include (e.g., writing, drawing, problem solving) and provide the basis for their assessment.

9. The preparation and use of assessment instruments are more likely to be effective where the objectives and specific learning outcomes have been clearly stated, the appropriate assessment and scoring methods have been selected, the assessment instruments are understandable and easy to use by students, the assessment instruments are shared with students before instruction begins, and are used by students during instruction to assess their own learning progress.

10. When assessment instruments are based on well-stated intended learning outcomes they provide more comprehensive and valid evidence of student learning.

Appendix A

Checklist for Evaluating the Final List of Objectives

In this book we have described and illustrated how to identify and define instructional objectives in terms of student performance. Our focus was on the *stating* of the objectives and the specific learning outcomes. Questions such as "Which objectives are most desirable for a particular instructional unit?" we leave to the curriculum specialist and subject expert. In evaluating your final list of objectives, however, you might want to appraise the adequacy of the list, as well as how clearly the statements indicate your instructional intent. Therefore, general criteria for evaluating the final list of objectives and specific learning outcomes have been incorporated into this checklist.

The checklist is intended as a diagnostic tool for detecting and correcting errors in the final list of objectives. Any negative answer indicates an area where improvement is needed. The checklist is also useful, of course, as a guide for developing the original list of instructional objectives.

Checklist

Yes/No

Adequacy of the List of General Instructional Objectives

_____ 1. Does each general instructional objective indicate an appropriate outcome for the instructional unit? (See recommendations of curriculum and subject experts.)

_____ 2. Does the list of general instructional objectives include all logical outcomes of the unit (knowledge, comprehension, application, skills, attitudes, and so on)?

_____ 3. Are the general instructional objectives attainable (do they take into account the ability of the students, facilities, time available, and so on)?

_____ 4. Are the general instructional objectives in harmony with the philosophy of the school?

_____ 5. Are the general instructional objectives in harmony with sound principles of learning (e.g., are the outcomes those that are most permanent and transferrable)?

Statements of General Instructional Objectives

_____ 6. Does each general instructional objective begin with a *verb* (e.g., knows, comprehends, appreciates)?

_____ 7. Is each general instructional objective stated in terms of *student performance* (rather than teacher performance)?

_____ 8. Is each general instructional objective stated as a learning product (rather than in terms of the learning process)?

_____ 9. Is each general instructional objective stated in terms of the students' *terminal performance* (rather than the subject matter to be covered)?

_____ 10. Does each general instructional objective include only one general learning outcome?

_____ 11. Is each general instructional objective stated at the proper level of generality (i.e., is it clear, concise, and readily definable)?

_____ 12. Is each general instructional objective stated so that it is relatively independent (i.e., free from overlap with other objectives)?

Statements of Specific Learning Outcomes

_____ 13. Is each general instructional objective defined by a list of specific learning outcomes that describes the types of performance students are expected to demonstrate?

_____ 14. Does each specific learning outcome begin with a *verb* that specifies definite, *observable performance* (e.g., identifies, describes, lists)?

_____ 15. Is the performance described in each specific learning outcome relevant to the general instructional objective?

_____ 16. Is there a sufficient number of specific learning outcomes to describe adequately the performance of students who have achieved each of the general instructional objectives?

_____ 17. Is each specific learning outcome stated so that it can be used with various units of study?

_____ 18. Is each specific learning outcome appropriate for the area and level of instruction?

Taxonomy of Educational Objectives (Major Categories and Illustrative Objectives)

Table B.1   Major Categories in the Cognitive Domain of the Taxonomy of Educational Objectives

Descriptions of the Major Categories in the Cognitive Domain

1. **Knowledge.** Knowledge is defined as the remembering of previously learned material. This may involve the recall of a wide range of material, from specific facts to complete theories, but all that is required is the bringing to mind of the appropriate information. Knowledge represents the lowest level of learning outcomes in the cognitive domain.

2. **Comprehension.** Comprehension is defined as the ability to grasp the meaning of material. This may be shown by translating material from one form to another (words to numbers), by interpreting material (explaining or summarizing), and by estimating future trends (predicting consequences or effects). These learning outcomes go one step beyond the simple remembering of material, and represent the lowest level of understanding.

3. **Application.** Application refers to the ability to use learned material in new and concrete situations. This may include the application of such things as rules, methods, concepts, principles, laws, and theories. Learning outcomes in this area require a higher level of understanding than those under comprehension.

4. **Analysis.** Analysis refers to the ability to break down material into its component parts so that its organizational structure may be understood. This may include the identification of the parts, analysis of the relationships between parts, and recognition of the organizational principles involved. Learning outcomes here represent a higher intellectual level than comprehension and application because they require an understanding of both the content and the structural form of the material.

5. **Synthesis.** Synthesis refers to the ability to put parts together to form a new whole. This may involve the production of a unique communication (theme or speech), a plan of operations (research proposal), or a set of abstract relations (scheme for classifying information). Learning outcomes in this area stress creative behaviors, with major emphasis on the formulation of *new* patterns of structures.

6. **Evaluation.** Evaluation is concerned with the ability to judge the value of material (statement, novel, poem, research report) for a given purpose. The judgments are to be based on definite criteria. These may be internal criteria (organization) or external criteria (relevance to the purpose), and the student may determine the criteria or be given them. Learning outcomes in this area are highest in the cognitive hierarchy because they contain elements of all of the other categories, plus conscious value judgments based on clearly defined criteria.

Illustrative General Instructional Objectives	Illustrative Verbs for Stating Specific Learning Outcomes
Knows common terms Knows specific facts Knows methods and procedures Knows basic concepts Knows principles	Defines, describes, identifies, labels, lists, matches, names, outlines, reproduces, selects, states
Comprehends facts and principles Interprets verbal material Interprets charts and graphs Translates verbal material to mathematical formulas Estimates future consequences implied in data Justifies methods and procedures	Converts, defends, distinguishes, estimates, explains, extends, generalizes, gives examples, infers, paraphrases, predicts, rewrites, summarizes
Applies concepts and principles to new situations Applies laws and theories to practical situations Solves mathematical problems Constructs charts and graphs Demonstrates correct usage of a method or procedure	Changes, computes, demonstrates, discovers, manipulates, modifies, operates, predicts, prepares, produces, relates, shows, solves, uses
Recognizes unstated assumptions Recognizes logical fallacies in reasoning Distinguishes between facts and inferences Evaluates the relevancy of data Analyzes the organizational structure of a work (art, music, writing)	Breaks down, diagrams, differentiates, discriminates, distinguishes, identifies, illustrates, infers, outlines, points out, relates, selects, separates, subdivides
Writes a well-organized theme Gives a well-organized speech Writes a creative short story (or poem, or music) Proposes a plan for an experiment Integrates learning from different areas into a plan for solving a problem Formulates a new scheme for classifying objects (or events, or ideas)	Categorizes, combines, compiles, composes, creates, devises, designs, explains, generates, modifies, organizes, plans, rearranges, reconstructs, relates, reorganizes, revises, rewrites, summarizes, tells, writes
Judges the logical consistency of written material Judges the adequacy with which conclusions are supported by data Judges the value of a work (art, music, writing) by use of internal criteria Judges the value of a work (art, music, writing) by use of external standards of excellence	Appraises, compares, concludes, contrasts, criticizes, describes, discriminates, explains, justifies, interprets, relates, summarizes, supports

Note: Material in first column (p. 112) from *Taxonomy of Educational Objectives: Handbook I, Cognitive Domain*, by B. S. Bloom, M. D. Englehart, E. J. Furst, W. H. Hill, & D. R. Krathwohl, 1956, New York: David McKay. Adapted with permission.

Table B.2   Major Categories in the Affective Domain of the Taxonomy of Educational Objectives

---

Descriptions of the Major Categories in the Affective Domain

1. **Receiving.** Receiving refers to the student's willingness to attend to particular phenomena or stimuli (classroom activities, textbook, music, etc.). From a teaching standpoint, it is concerned with getting, holding, and directing the student's attention. Learning outcomes in this area range from the simple awareness that a thing exists to selective attention on the part of the learner. Receiving represents the lowest level of learning outcomes in the affective domain.

2. **Responding.** Responding refers to active participation on the part of the student. At this level he or she not only attends to a particular phenomenon but also reacts to it in some way. Learning outcomes in this area may emphasize acquiescence in responding (reads assigned material), willingness to respond (voluntarily reads beyond assignment), or satisfaction in responding (reads for pleasure or enjoyment). The higher levels of this category include those instructional objectives that are commonly classified under "interest"; that is, those that stress the seeking out and enjoyment of particular activities.

3. **Valuing.** Valuing is concerned with the worth or value a student attaches to a particular object, phenomenon, or behavior. This ranges in degree from the more simple acceptance of a value (desires to improve group skills) to the more complex level of commitment (assumes responsibility for the effective functioning of the group). Valuing is based on the internalization of a set of specified values, but clues to these values are expressed in the student's overt behavior. Learning outcomes in this area are concerned with behavior that is consistent and stable enough to make the value clearly identifiable. Instructional objectives that are commonly classified under "attitudes" and "appreciation" would fall into this category.

4. **Organization.** Organization is concerned with bringing together different values, resolving conflicts between them, and beginning the building of an internally consistent value system. Thus the emphasis is on comparing, relating, and synthesizing values. Learning outcomes may be concerned with the conceptualization of a value (recognizes the responsibility of each individual for improving human relations) or with the organization of a value system (develops a vocational plan that satisfies his or her need for both economic security and social service). Instructional objectives relating to the development of a philosophy of life would fall into this category.

5. **Characterization by a Value or Value Complex.** At this level of the affective domain the individual has a value system that has controlled his or her behavior for a sufficiently long time for him or her to have developed a characteristic "life-style." Thus the behavior is pervasive, consistent, and predictable. Learning outcomes at this level cover a broad range of activities, but the major emphasis is on the fact that the behavior is typical or characteristic of the student. Instructional objectives that are concerned with the student's general patterns of adjustment (personal, social, emotional) would be appropriate here.

Illustrative General Instructional Objectives	Illustrative Verbs for Stating Specific Learning Outcomes
Listens attentively Shows awareness of the importance of learning Shows sensitivity to human needs and social problems Accepts differences of race and culture Attends closely to the classroom activities	Asks, chooses, describes, follows, gives, holds, identifies, locates, names, points to, replies, selects, sits erect, uses
Completes assigned homework Obeys school rules Participates in class discussion Completes laboratory work Volunteers for special tasks Shows interest in subject Enjoys helping others	Answers, assists, complies, conforms, discusses, greets, helps, labels, performs, practices, presents, reads, recites, reports, selects, tells, writes
Demonstrates belief in the democratic process Appreciates good literature (art or music) Appreciates the role of science (or other subjects) in everyday life Shows concern for the welfare of others Demonstrates problem-solving attitude Demonstrates commitment to social improvement	Completes, describes, differentiates, explains, follows, forms, initiates, invites, joins, justifies, proposes, reads, reports, selects, shares, studies, works
Recognizes the need for balance between freedom and responsibility in a democracy Recognizes the role of systematic planning in solving problems Accepts responsibility for his or her own behavior Understands and accepts his or her own strengths and limitations Formulates life plan in harmony with his or her abilities, interests, and beliefs	Adheres, alters, arranges, combines, compares, completes, defends, explains, generalizes, identifies, integrates, modifies, orders, organizes, prepares, relates, synthesizes
Displays safety consciousness Demonstrates self-reliance working independently Practices cooperation in group activities Uses objective approach in problem solving Demonstrates industry, punctuality, and self-discipline Maintains good health habits	Acts, discriminates, displays, influences, listens, modifies, performs, practices, proposes, qualifies, questions, revises, serves, solves, uses, verifies

Note: Material in first column (p. 114) from *Taxonomy of Educational Objectives: Handbook II, Affective Domain*, by D. R. Krathwohl, B. S. Bloom, & B. B. Masia, 1964, New York: David McKay. Adapted with permission.

Table B.3   A Classification of Educational Objectives in the Psychomotor Domain

---

Descriptions of the Major Categories in the Psychomotor Domain

---

1. **Perception.** The first level is concerned with the use of the sense organs to obtain cues that guide motor activity. This category ranges from sensory stimulation (awareness of a stimulus), through cue selection (selecting task-relevant cues), to translation (relating cue perception to action in a performance).

---

2. **Set.** Set refers to readiness to take a particular type of action. This category includes mental set (mental readiness to act), physical set (physical readiness to act), and emotional set (willingness to act). Perception of cues serves as an important prerequisite for this level.

---

3. **Guided Response.** Guided response is concerned with the early stages in learning a complex skill. It includes imitation (repeating an act demonstrated by the instructor) and trial and error (using a multiple-response approach to identify an appropriate response). Adequacy of performance is judged by an instructor or by a suitable set of criteria.

---

4. **Mechanism.** Mechanism is concerned with performance acts where the learned responses have become habitual and the movements can be performed with some confidence and proficiency. Learning outcomes at this level are concerned with performance skills of various types, but the movement patterns are less complex than at the next higher level.

---

5. **Complex Overt Response.** Complex overt response is concerned with the skillful performance of motor acts that involve complex movement patterns. Proficiency is indicated by a quick, smooth, accurate performance, requiring a minimum of energy. This category includes resolution of uncertainty (performs without hesitation) and automatic performance (movements are made with ease and good muscle control). Learning outcomes at this level include highly coordinated motor activities.

---

6. **Adaptation.** Adaptation is concerned with skills that are so well developed that the individual can modify movement patterns to fit special requirements or to meet a problem situation.

---

7. **Origination.** Origination refers to the creating of new movement patterns to fit a particular situation or specific problem. Learning outcomes at this level emphasize creativity based upon highly developed skills.

Illustrative General Instructional Objectives	Illustrative Verbs for Stating Specific Learning Outcomes
Recognizes malfunction by sound of machine Relates taste of food to need for seasoning Relates music to a particular dance step	Chooses, describes, detects, differentiates, distinguishes, identifies, isolates, relates, selects, separates
Knows sequence of steps in varnishing wood Demonstrates proper bodily stance for batting a ball Shows desire to type efficiently	Begins, displays, explains, moves, proceeds, reacts, responds, shows, starts, volunteers
Performs a golf swing as demonstrated Applies first-aid bandage as demonstrated Determines best sequence for preparing a meal	Assembles, builds, calibrates, constructs, dismantles, displays, dissects, fastens, fixes, grinds, heats, manipulates, measures, mends, mixes, organizes, sketches, works
Writes smoothly and legibly Sets up laboratory equipment Operates a slide projector Demonstrates a simple dance step	(Same list as for Guided Response)
Operates a power saw skillfully Demonstrates correct form in swimming Demonstrates skill in driving an automobile Performs skillfully on the violin Repairs electronic equipment quickly and accurately	(Same list as for Guided Response)
Adjusts tennis play to counteract opponent's style Modifies swimming strokes to fit the roughness of the water	Adapts, alters, changes, rearranges, reorganizes, revises, varies
Creates a dance step Creates a musical composition Designs a new dress style	Arranges, combines, composes, constructs, designs, originates

Note: Material in first column (p. 116) from *The Classification of Educational Objectives in the Psychomotor Domain*, by E. J. Simpson, 1972, Washington, DC: Gryphon House. Adapted with permission.

Appendix C

Illustrative Verbs

Illustrative Verbs for Stating General Instructional Objectives

Analyze	Compute	Interpret	Perform	Translate
Apply	Create	Know	Recognize	Understand
Appreciate	Demonstrate	Listen	Speak	Use
Comprehend	Evaluate	Locate	Think	Write

Illustrative Verbs for Stating Specific Learning Outcomes[1]

"Creative" Behaviors

Alter	Paraphrase	Reconstruct	Rephrase	Rewrite
Ask	Predict	Regroup	Restate	Simplify
Change	Question	Rename	Restructure	Synthesize
Design	Rearrange	Reorder	Retell	Systematize
Generalize	Recombine	Reorganize	Revise	Vary
Modify				

Complex, Logical, Judgmental Behaviors

Analyze	Conclude	Deduce	Formulate	Plan
Appraise	Contrast	Defend	Generate	Structure
Combine	Criticize	Evaluate	Induce	Substitute
Compare	Decide	Explain	Infer	

[1]This list was developed by Calvin K. Claus, Psychology Department, National College of Education, Evanston, Ill. Printed by permission from a paper presented at the annual meeting of the National Council on Measurement in Education (Chicago: February, 1968). It provides a useful collection of verbs for the beginner.

General Discriminative Behaviors

Choose	Detect	Identify	Match	Place
Collect	Differentiate	Indicate	Omit	Point
Define	Discriminate	Isolate	Order	Select
Describe	Distinguish	List	Pick	Separate

Social Behaviors

Accept	Communicate	Discuss	Invite	Praise
Agree	Compliment	Excuse	Join	React
Aid	Contribute	Forgive	Laugh	Smile
Allow	Cooperate	Greet	Meet	Talk
Answer	Dance	Help	Participate	Thank
Argue	Disagree	Interact	Permit	Volunteer

Language Behaviors

Abbreviate	Edit	Punctuate	Speak	Tell
Accent	Hyphenate	Read	Spell	Translate
Alphabetize	Indent	Recite	State	Verbalize
Articulate	Outline	Say	Summarize	Whisper
Call	Print	Sign	Syllabify	Write
Capitalize	Pronounce			

"Study" Behaviors

Arrange	Compile	Itemize	Mark	Record
Categorize	Copy	Label	Name	Reproduce
Chart	Diagram	Locate	Note	Search
Circle	Find	Look	Organize	Sort
Cite	Follow	Map	Quote	Underline

Music Behaviors

Blow	Compose	Hum	Pluck	Strum
Bow	Finger	Mute	Practice	Tap
Clap	Harmonize	Play	Sing	Whistle

Physical Behaviors

Arch	Face	Jump	Push	Step
Bat	Float	Kick	Run	Stretch
Bend	Grab	Knock	Skate	Swim
Carry	Grasp	Lift	Ski	Swing
Catch	Grip	March	Skip	Throw
Chase	Hit	Pitch	Somersault	Toss
Climb	Hop	Pull	Stand	Walk

Arts Behaviors

Assemble	Dot	Illustrate	Press	Stamp
Blend	Draw	Melt	Roll	Stick
Brush	Drill	Mix	Rub	Stir
Build	Fold	Mold	Sand	Trace
Carve	Form	Nail	Saw	Trim
Color	Frame	Paint	Sculpt	Varnish
Construct	Hammer	Paste	Shake	Wipe
Cut	Handle	Pat	Sketch	Wrap
Dab	Heat	Pour	Smooth	

Drama Behaviors

Act	Display	Express	Pass	Show
Clasp	Emit	Leave	Perform	Sit
Cross	Enter	Move	Proceed	Start
Direct	Exit	Pantomime	Respond	Turn

Mathematical Behaviors

Add	Derive	Group	Number	Square
Bisect	Divide	Integrate	Plot	Subtract
Calculate	Estimate	Interpolate	Prove	Tabulate
Check	Extrapolate	Measure	Reduce	Tally
Compute	Extract	Multiply	Solve	Verify
Count	Graph			

Laboratory Science Behaviors

Apply	Demonstrate	Keep	Prepare	Specify
Calibrate	Dissect	Lengthen	Remove	Straighten
Conduct	Feed	Limit	Replace	Time
Connect	Grow	Manipulate	Report	Transfer
Convert	Increase	Operate	Reset	Weigh
Decrease	Insert	Plant	Set	

General Appearance, Health, and Safety Behaviors

Button	Dress	Fasten	Taste	Unzip
Clean	Drink	Fill	Tie	Wait
Clear	Eat	Go	Unbutton	Wash
Close	Eliminate	Lace	Uncover	Wear
Comb	Empty	Stop	Untie	Zip
Cover				

Miscellaneous

Aim	Erase	Lead	Relate	Stake
Attempt	Expand	Lend	Repeat	Start
Attend	Extend	Let	Return	Stock
Begin	Feel	Light	Ride	Store
Bring	Finish	Make	Rip	Strike
Buy	Fit	Mend	Save	Suggest
Come	Fix	Miss	Scratch	Supply
Complete	Flip	Offer	Send	Support
Consider	Get	Open	Serve	Switch
Correct	Give	Pack	Sew	Take
Crease	Grind	Pay	Share	Tear
Crush	Guide	Peel	Sharpen	Touch
Designate	Hand	Pin	Shoot	Try
Determine	Hang	Position	Shorten	Twist
Develop	Hold	Present	Shovel	Type
Discover	Hook	Produce	Shut	Use
Distribute	Hunt	Propose	Signify	Vote
Do	Include	Provide	Slide	Watch
Drop	Inform	Put	Slip	Weave
End	Lay	Raise	Spread	Work

Appendix D

References

Bloom, B. S. (Ed.), Englehart, M. D., Furst, E. J., Hill, W. H., & Krathwohl, D. R. (1956). *Taxonomy of Educational Objectives: Handbook I, Cognitive Domain*. New York: David McKay. Describes the cognitive categories in detail and presents illustrative objectives and test items for each.

Gagné, R. M. (1985). *The Conditions of Learning and Theory of Instruction* (4th ed.). New York: Holt, Rinehart, & Winston. Describes a framework for classifying learning outcomes.

Gronlund, N. E. (1998). *Assessment of Student Achievement* (6th ed.). Boston: Allyn Bacon. Describes and illustrates how to construct test items and various assessment procedures.

Harrow, A. J. (1972). *A Taxonomy of the Psychomotor Domain*. New York: David McKay. Provides a model for classifying learning outcomes in the psychomotor domain and presents illustrative objectives.

Krathwohl, D. R., Bloom, B. S., & Masia, B. B. (1964). *Taxonomy of Educational Objectives: Handbook II, Affective Domain*. New York: David McKay. Describes the affective categories in detail and presents illustrative objectives and test items for each.

Linn, R. L., & Gronlund, N. E. (2000). *Measurement and Assessment in Teaching* (8th ed.). Upper Saddle River, NJ: Merrill/Prentice Hall. A textbook that describes the process of preparing instructional objectives and using them in testing and assessing student learning.

Marzano, R. J., Brandt, R. S., Hughes, C. S., Jones, B. F., Presseisen, B. Z., Rankin, S. C., & Suhor, C. (1988). *Dimensions of Thinking: A Framework for Curriculum and Instruction*. Alexandria, VA: Association for Supervision and Curriculum Development.

Mueller, D. J. (1986). *Measuring Social Attitudes*. New York: Teachers College Press. Describes and illustrates how to construct attitude scales.

Quellmalz, E. S. (1985). Developing Reasoning Skills. In J. R. Baron & R. J. Sternberg (Eds.), *Teaching Thinking Skills: Theory and Practice* (86–105). New York: Freeman. Describes a simple framework for classifying outcomes in the cognitive domain.

Simpson, E. J. (1972). "The Classification of Educational Objectives in the Psychomotor Domain." *The Psychomotor Domain* (Vol. 3). Washington, DC: Gryphon House. Describes the psychomotor domain in detail and presents illustrative objectives.

Stiggins, R. J., & Conklin, N. F. (1992). *In Teachers Hands: Investigating the Practices of Classroom Assessment.* Albany: State University of New York Press. A study of teachers' use of assessment procedures in assessing student learning.

Wiggins, G. (1998). *Educative Assessment.* San Francisco: Jossey-Bass Publisher. A practical guide for designing assessment instruments.

Index

125